# Incident at the Otterville Station

# Incident at the Otterville Station

## A Civil War Story of Slavery and Rescue

JOHN CHRISTGAU

*University of Nebraska Press*
*Lincoln and London*

Library of Congress Cataloging-in-Publication Data

Christgau, John.

Incident at the Otterville Station : a Civil War story of slavery and rescue / John Christgau.

pages cm

Includes bibliographical references.

ISBN 978-0-8032-4644-7 (pbk: alk. paper)

ISBN 978-0-8032-4937-0

ISBN 978-0-8032-4938-7 (mobi)

ISBN 978-0-8032-4872-4 (pdf)

1. Slaves—Emancipation—Missouri—Otterville. 2. United States. Army. Minnesota Infantry Regiment, 9th (1862–1865) 3. Missouri—History—Civil War, 1861–1865—Social aspects. 4. United States—History—Civil War, 1861–1865—Social aspects. 5. Otterville (Mo.)—History—19th century. 6. Mutiny—Missouri—Otterville. I. Title.

E453.C49 2013

973.7'478—dc23

2013025405

Set in SwiftEF by Laura Wellington.

# Contents

# Acknowledgments

I am grateful to numerous people, organizations, and archives for their help in reconstructing the events surrounding the incident at the Otterville station:

Sue Doocy and the Mower County Historical Society; Marianne Mastenbrook and the Laird Lucas Memorial Library and Archives in Winona; Bill Creech, Carlton Barnes, and Rodney Ross of the National Archives; Austin Public Library; Minnesota Historical Society; Lauren Leeman and Kimberly Harper and the State Historical Society of Missouri; Elizabeth Engel and Susan Hart and the Western Historical Manuscript Collection; Missouri State Archives; Missouri Department of Health and Senior Services; Pettis County Historical Society; Jefferson City Historical Society; Anne Gue and the Cole County Historical Society; Cooper County Historical Society; Pettis County Recorder's Office; Cornell University Library; Federal Archives and Record Center in San Bruno, California; California Historical Society; San Mateo County Library; Mower County Recorder's Office; Oakland and Greenwood Cemeteries, Mower County, Minnesota; Dr. Steve Fox; Sheryl McClure and the Freeborn County Historical Society; Leon Basile; Mike Schuth; genealogists Mary Lindbo, Alex Early,

Keith Daleen, Cheryl Sears, Bryant Walker, Kris Marshall, Gene Queen, Tom Pearson, James Thoma, George Willick, and Annette Curtis Klause. Finally, Jerry Anderson planted the seed for the story, and Jim Hanson of Grand Meadow and the late Dr. Roger Christgau of Austin helped me to see how the land lays in Mower County.

# CHAPTER 1

# The Great Emancipator

The grandest ball in the history of this country was held on an unusually warm Thursday night in November of 1863 in New York City. Following some of the heaviest fighting of the Civil War, thousands of guests promenaded into the Great Russian Ball along a narrow walkway of magenta carpet at the New York Academy of Music. Bronze statues holding lighted torches flanked the entry doors to the dance floor. White tapestries and baskets with braided ropes of bright flowers hung along the walls.

On the huge dance floor, what was described as a mass of humanity heaved and flowed. Dancers struggled to find room to step and whirl. There were waltzes and quadrilles and polkas. Actors, empresses, soldiers, writers, statesmen, beautiful young women in magnificent dresses garnished with pomegranate blossoms and sparkling dew drop diamonds looped and glided and bumped. The ballroom smelled of thick perfumes and forget-me-nots. The music of Rossini and Verdi and Schubert glided above the steady hum of the cheerful voices of the dancers.

Two and a half years had passed since Confederate forces had fired on Fort Sumter in April of 1861 and set off a bloody Civil War. The war would be a brief one, President Lincoln thought, to put down a Southern rebellion. Some insisted the war was about preserving the Union while others claimed it was over the issue of slavery. "If slavery is not wrong," Lincoln said, "nothing is wrong."

Whatever the causes, Lincoln had called for the formation of a militia to put down the rebellion. Ninety thousand men signed up as three-month volunteers. But after the rebel victory in July of 1861 at the First Battle of Bull Run, it was obvious that there would be no quick end to the war.

A critical Union victory in September of 1862 at Antietam, Maryland, restored Union hopes. Dead soldiers from both the Union and Confederate armies lay scattered and heaped along the rail fences of the battlefield, but Northern newspapers wrote, "At no time have the hopes of the nation been so close to realization."

Two months later, in what was described as a "strange and terrible" battle at Fredericksburg, Virginia, the rebels proved too much for Union forces. During the battle, Union soldiers made their way forward through the bodies of their fallen comrades, spaced in death with the order of railroad ties. One Union soldier wrote that it was "a masterly piece of butchery . . . with not a thing accomplished." Northerners were outraged, and the Union's hope for victory sank again.

After a week of bloody battle in May of 1863, at a crossroads in Virginia called Chancellorsville, Union forces suffered nearly twenty thousand casualties. It was more senseless butchery with nothing resolved. But two months later, Northern spirits soared again after Union forces at Gettysburg rained cannon balls and bullets from the high ground of Cemetery Ridge on rebel forces marching with fixed bayonets through bucolic wheat fields and peach orchards and a valley of death sprinkled with wildflowers.

The Union victory at Gettysburg was still a cause for celebration when those revelers and exhausted dancers in New York City sat down late at night to consume a seven course banquet featuring half a ton of beef and a thousand ducklings prepared as *canetons a la rouennaise.* Then a thousand champagne corks exploded like the gunfire in a war that was still raging, and a toast was proposed to "Abraham Lincoln the Great Emancipator."

The dancers had hardly recovered from the gala event when, a thousand miles across the country, a Missouri slave owner named Charles W. Walker in Pettis County gathered his thirteen sleepy slaves in the middle of the night in front of their cabin. The cold air held no trace of the intoxicating perfumes of dancers. The squawks of roosters replaced the strains of Strauss and Verdi. There were no bright lights or sparkling diamonds, no pomegranate blossoms. Instead of the savory aroma of roast ducklings, there was only the sharp smell of fried fatback and barnyard manure. Instead of a thousand cheerful voices, there was only the lone, flat voice of Master Walker as he addressed his assembled slaves of six adults and seven small children.

He had awakened them early, he wanted them to know, because he was shipping them by train that morning to Kentucky, where they were to be sold on the slave market in Louisville.

The thirteen slaves were stunned. Walker often worked the fields of his farm beside his slaves. He had always been kindly and sociable. Meanwhile, Missouri was surrounded by free territory that invited runaways. Walker knew as well as anyone that cruelty to slaves only increased the possibility of flight.

That flight had been going on for decades. Tens of thousands of slaves had fled to Canada by virtue of the underground railroad, which seems to suggest escaping like burrowing moles. But the "railroad" was neither subterranean nor confined to tracks, instead following along secret trails from one safe house to another. The runaway slaves slept in barns by day and traveled mostly by foot or wagon at night, until they reached Canada. In an effort to discourage the flight, slave owners warned that escape to Yankee safety would mean neglect and abuse. Or they warned that the fugitives were a threat to Yankee peace and order. But how could penniless Negroes armed with nothing but corn cutters and clubs threaten anybody?

Predictions of slaves making war against the Yankees and warnings by slave owners of Yankee cruelty did not discourage flight. Once the Civil War began, the chaos of battle presented opportunities for escape to nearby Union lines. Among slaves, word of mouth about the possibility of escape to the Union lines encouraged still more flights to freedom. On the East Coast, fleeing slaves commandeered rowboats and barges, then made their way across bays and inlets and along creeks and narrows to find refuge on Union naval vessels. Slave owners complained of the slaves' "stampede to the enemy." The inland was crisscrossed with runaway trails. Meanwhile, in the months before Charles Walker faced his slaves in the barnyard dark, slave owners like him had sent a thousand slaves to be sold in the slave auctions of Kentucky.

Standing before his slaves, Walker did not bother to explain how the national controversy over slavery was threatening his way of life in Missouri. While mighty forces of the split nation clashed at dirt crossroads at Chancellorsville and in wheat fields at Gettysburg, Missouri became a battle ground on a smaller scale for those same forces, at places like Boonville and Wilson's Creek.

The Missouri Compromise of 1820 was meant to be national legislation that would settle the issue of whether new states would be admitted to the Union as free or slave. Missouri was eventually admitted as a slave state, but the quarrel over the fate of new states did not disappear. Now those same forces that whipsawed the North and the South between hopes for glorious victory and despair over senseless butchery had split Missouri into bitter factions. However, there was no clear line separating the two factions. On the farms and in the villages and cities within the state, families split and neighbor fought against neighbor over the issues of secession and slavery.

The fight between the two warring factions in Missouri was every bit as passionate and often bloody as the clashes on the battlefields of Fredericksburg and Antietam. Even before the fighting started in the East, Missouri's governor Claiborne Jackson, who spoke of Missouri's "sisterhood" with slave states, organized the various militias of the state into a Missouri state guard that would serve as a military arm for those Missouri citizens who favored the preservation of slavery and secession from the Union. "Throw off the yoke of the North," one of the commanders urged.

Early in 1861 a state convention of politicians rejected the idea of secession. Their decision wasn't solely an expression of antislavery sentiments. Much of Missouri's commerce and grain trade depended on eastern markets. Secession would deprive Missouri of those markets and end the state's control of the Missouri and Mississippi River corridors along which that trade moved. Seceding from the Union would be tantamount to an act of self-destruction.

After the firing on Fort Sumter, President Lincoln's call for 75,000 militia men created outrage in parts of Missouri. Governor Jackson and ardent rebel sympathizers refused the call from the Union for Missouri militiamen to help put down the Southern rebellion. The move appeared to favor the Confederacy and slaveholding in Missouri. But over the preceding decades, the character of the state had changed. There had been an explosion of white immigrants. The immigrants, many of whom were Germans who objected to slavery, were emerging as a new political force. The influence of those who felt that slavery was an economic necessity and a cultural way of life was declining.

Missouri politicians and others, including abolitionists, offered to create a "Home Guard" militia that would accept rather than reject the federal government's call to arms. Meanwhile, Governor Jackson met secretly with secessionists to lay plans for a force drawn from various militia units in the state to seize the federal arsenal in St. Louis. Confederate states offered to send troops to help carry out Jackson's plan.

The plan failed when Union troops surrounded what was called "Camp Jackson" and placed Jackson and his men under arrest. Riots in St. Louis over federal intervention and the arrest of Jackson's men created still deeper division within the state. Jackson called for fifty thousand young Missouri men to take up arms against the tyranny of the United States.

Just when it appeared that the secessionists would prevail in Missouri, Jackson was forced to flee the state capitol at Jefferson City and form a government in exile in Boonville, Missouri. Jackson's government had no territory to administer and few civic duties to carry out. The Union forces in Missouri took heart again and declared that Jackson had expatriated himself. A provisional state government was hastily formed in Jefferson City. Delegates to another state convention elected Hamilton Gamble as provisional governor. If Unionists expected the new governor to make the threat of rebellion disappear, they were quickly disappointed. It is "utterly impossible that any one man can pacify the troubled waters of the state," Gamble said at his inauguration.

In efforts to keep the peace, one of the Union's first military skirmishes was a brief fight against Jackson's newly formed state guard defending his government in exile in Boonville. Jackson and his troops were quickly routed, and Jackson headed for his second exile, this time in southwestern Missouri.

The pendulum had swung back in favor of the Union again. With Jackson in exile and his state guard forces defeated, pro-Confederates in central Missouri who were eager to fight had two choices: leave the state or join various guerilla organizations. Many chose the latter, and guerilla insurgents adopted hit-and-run tactics, harassing Union troops, burning bridges, and attacking supply trains. These attacks meant that train engines had to be fitted with bulletproof iron plates. Boxcar doors were removed so that Union troops could quickly jump out and shoot.

The guerillas, or "bushwhackers," so named because they whacked their way through thick bushes and heavy woods with machetes, were a haphazard but pesky enemy that saw itself as a critical force in the fight to resist Missouri Unionists. President Lincoln appointed General John Fremont to lead federal forces in northern Missouri against the bushwhackers. Lincoln promised Fremont all the military resources he would need to clear the state of guerillas and rebels. Once again, rebel sympathizers in Missouri seemed to be on the run.

But General Fremont's first Draconian moves in Missouri were to declare that all slaves of masters disloyal to the Union were free. He imposed martial law first on St. Louis, then on the entire state. The dramatic action created an outcry from the state's slaveholders and citizens. Jackson's government in exile quickly passed an ordinance calling for secession. Meanwhile, radical Missouri abolitionists cheered Fremont's dramatic approach.

Lincoln hoped to keep Missouri and the loyal border states of Kentucky, Delaware, and Maryland in the Union. Those states all clung to the institution of slavery, and their attachment to the Union was precarious. Provoking a confrontation with any of them over the issue of slavery might turn them against the Union and drive them into the Confederacy. That eventuality would undermine the Union and give the Confederacy more manpower and resources to fight the war.

Taking a position that he hoped struck a middle ground between abolition and secession, Lincoln argued for a gradual and less antagonistic approach in loyal border states. His idea was that the owners of slaves could be persuaded to give up slavery if they were *compensated* for the release of their slaves. Now General Fremont's actions in Missouri, freeing all slaves of owners who were disloyal to the Union, were abrupt and provocative. As 1861 ended, Lincoln countermanded Fremont's order and relieved him of his command. The general's military career in Missouri had lasted just one hundred days.

Despite 52,000 new federal troops in Missouri, the guerillas refused to go away, particularly in seven counties along the Missouri River valley in a region called Little Dixie. The farmers there were mostly migrants from Virginia and Kentucky who in the decades prior to the Civil War had settled the region because the land was cheap and the Missouri bottomlands were fertile. Tobacco crops and particularly the backbreaking labor of hemp production meant that over a third of the region's inhabitants were slaves who were the backbone of the state's slave labor. Although the slaveholders were farmers with only half as many slaves per household as the plantations of the Deep South, they and the citizens of Little Dixie considered themselves Southern, and many harbored secession sentiments. Meanwhile, the area had a long history of militancy; and with the start of the Civil War and Lincoln's call for troops, Little Dixie became a hotbed of anti-Union sentiment. The area was the perfect breeding ground for the insurrection that led to guerilla warfare in every corner of Little Dixie not long after the start of the war.

Who were these outlaws who were blowing up railroad bridges and terrifying the citizens into abandoning farms with crops rotting in the fields? They were "white trash," their opponents insisted. They were nothing but outlaws, bandits, and horse thieves. They were cowardly and wolf-like. They scalped Union soldiers. They were pirates, gangsters, murderers, and robbers who glorified terror. Their ranks included some of the most psychopathic killers and bandits in U.S. history, among them the Younger brothers and Frank James. They were enemies of Christianity who were without principle. Finally, they were worthless in true battle.

In fact, they were not as trashy and villainous as their opponents insisted. They came mainly from farms and villages. They may have sympathized with the South, but most had been born in Missouri. They were typically the eldest sons of wealthy farm families who owned numerous slaves. As the eldest sons, likely to inherit the wealth and property of their parents, they stood to lose more than anyone else if slavery was abolished in Missouri. In the minds of their supporters, they were noble and heroic figures who had risen to protect their families against savage aliens from the North.

However heroic the guerillas appeared to some, Union armies insisted they were not entitled to treatment as noble warriors, and in April of 1863 a German American jurist named Francis Lieber drew up a code of conduct that dictated how Union soldiers should behave in the field. Lieber's code, eventually signed by President Lincoln, characterized guerillas as brigands who committed ambush, devastation, rapine, robbery, and destruction. If caught on the battlefield, they could be summarily executed. Furthermore, the code argued that all men were equal and slavery existed only through municipal law. According to Lieber's code, slaves who fled their masters were free men and their masters had no right to claim them.

Lieber's code did little to change guerilla hit-and-run tactics. They struck quickly and unexpectedly, then disappeared into the Missouri woods. They continued to attack Union encampments and supply trains. They threatened the wives of Union supporters, they ransacked and burned homes, they stole food. Thousands of Union troops assigned to protect bridges and supply lines and telegraph lines were tied down in Missouri when they could have been used elsewhere.

The worst of the guerillas, or the most ingenious, some argued, was William Clarke Quantrill, the twenty-four-year-old ex-schoolteacher who seemed to be able to operate on the Missouri-Kansas border with impunity. At dawn on August 21, 1863, he led five hundred men fifty miles across the border into Kansas, where they made a surprise attack on Lawrence, Kansas, a base of operations for abolitionists. On the streets or in front of their families in their homes, 150 men and boys from the town were shot. After Quantrill and his men set fire to most of the town, they fled back into Missouri.

The cry in Kansas for vengeance was immediate. But Quantrill and his men had disappeared into the thick Missouri woods. There was little that could be done to him directly. But Union commanders were convinced that the guerilla bands could survive only with the assistance and forage provided by Confederate sympathizers in Missouri; and just four days after Quantrill's raid on Lawrence, Union General Thomas Ewing ordered the evacuation of four rural counties along the Kansas-Missouri border where the guerillas were wreaking havoc. Ewing's General Order no. 11, with President Lincoln's approval, was meant to deprive the guerillas of their material support, but the four counties became a no-man's-land where the raiders enjoyed even greater freedom to forage for food and supplies.

Meanwhile, Confederate forces had been making periodic forays into Missouri since the start of the war, hoping to recruit rebel soldiers, draw Union troops away from other battles, and bring Missouri into the Confederacy. However, rebel commanders complained to their superiors that they needed more troops to prevail in Missouri. Eventually, rebel forces that might have brought Missouri into the Confederacy and preserved slavery were routed.

For Charles Walker in Pettis County, that no-man's-land along the Missouri-Kansas border was too close to home. The hit-and-run tactics of the guerillas, however heroic, had been counterproductive. Radical abolitionist sentiments in Missouri had only grown stronger. Those radicals became so confident of their cause that they held an abolition convention. It was clear to Walker that the institution of slavery in Missouri was doomed.

In the predawn dark, he announced his intention to ship his slaves to one of the slave marts in Kentucky and sell them. His authorization to do so, he said, would come from the Union forces in Sedalia. For the thirteen slaves gathered in the dark, it meant that Abraham Lincoln was not the Great Emancipator who would ultimately control their fate and was being toasted in the ballrooms of New York. Their fate was in the immediate hands of their master, Charles W. Walker.

# CHAPTER 2

# Charles W. Walker

Charles W. Walker had been born in Casey County, Kentucky, in 1821, the second of thirteen children of a saddler named James T. Walker and his wife, Morning. In search of cheap and fertile land, the whole family had left Kentucky to homestead a small farm in Pettis County, Missouri, in 1847. The party of two adults and thirteen children made a long wagon train of horses and mules that wended its way over ridges and through steep defiles to a "land such as God had promised to the ancient Israelites."

At first, the numerous strapping boys in the family served as the laborers for raising wheat and hemp and for baling cotton. But James T. Walker saw that slaveholders in Pettis County produced three times the crops of non-slavers, and he promptly acquired a sixteen-year-old slave named John. Other slaves soon followed, until they numbered six adult slaves who did the field work and cooked and cleaned in the Walker household.

One-by-one, the Walker sons and daughters moved out. Then the family patriarch James T. Walker died, leaving Charles, still single at thirty-nine, to run the farm. In 1860, inspired by the example of his brothers who had married and started their own farms, Charles Walker married Martha Thompson, a young woman half his age, and he began a family of his own.

Meanwhile, the fight in Missouri over the issue of slavery continued. Sensing an opportunity during the conflict for freedom, slaves fled from their owners, and some were conscripted as soldiers in the war effort. The value of slaves began to decline. The days of slave ownership in the state seemed numbered. As the Civil War raged, slave owners began transporting their "property" to solid slave states to sell at auction markets or to safely harbor until the bloody war had ended.

Charles Walker understood that slaves would soon be of no value whatsoever in Missouri. Now he told the thirteen figures who stood before him in the dark to gather whatever personal belongings they could carry with them. In a matter of only a few minutes, on one of the horse-drawn farm wagons driven by his brother, Walker would take them to the Pacific Railroad terminus in Sedalia. There, he would board them on the train and escort them on the journey to slave markets in Louisville. It didn't matter who Abraham Lincoln claimed he had emancipated, Walker finished. There was no use attempting to escape. If he didn't immediately shoot them himself, mounted Missouri guerillas would hunt them down and shoot them on sight.

Walker and his brother set out in the dark with his slaves on the two-mile ride into Sedalia. The town had been laid out only a few years earlier but hadn't prospered until 1861, when it became the end of the line for the Pacific Railroad carrying passengers from Sedalia to St. Louis along stretches of the Missouri River. As it moved east, the train made brief stops to deliver goods and take on passengers in the towns of Smithton, Otterville, Syracuse, Tipton, and Jefferson City.

To serve those travelers as well as settlers, Sedalia had two dozen businesses along Main Street selling groceries, drugs, meat, tin ware, and whiskey. When Walker and his slaves arrived, those businesses were all dark and the town's three thousand citizens were still asleep. Only the wooden water tank at the railroad depot was visible in the dark, watching over Sedalia like a sentinel.

Walker led his slaves past the offices of the Overland Stage and the livery stables to the cattle yard on the southwest part of town, where Union soldiers were stationed to protect Sedalia from bushwhackers and rebel incursions.

The practice of shipping slaves out of state to avoid the inevitable end of slavery was controversial. Only the day before Walker addressed his slaves, orders prohibiting the practice had been issued from the headquarters for the Union army's Department of Missouri in St. Louis. "No provost marshal or other officer in military service," the order read, "will permit any person to take slaves from Missouri to any other state."

The order, however, had not yet been received by the young lieutenant who served as assistant provost marshal for the Sedalia troops who were just then waking up for the day's duty. Walker sought out the lieutenant, who listened to Walker's explanation of what he intended to do. He promptly wrote out a permit and signed it with a flourish, then sent Walker and his slaves on their way to the Sedalia depot.

The only hotel in town was the Ives House, described as a "kennel for a pack of hounds." But the hotel had a long covered veranda that served as the platform for the railroad depot, and Walker ordered his slaves out of the farm wagon and onto the platform.

The locomotive engine sat in the dark like a horned black beast that had been watered and fed and now belched periodic clouds of steam from its sated iron belly. Behind the engine and its tender, two boxcars and a string of passenger coaches stretched down the track.

Walker presented his certificate of authorization to the platform agent, who read it carefully. "Permission is granted for Charles W. Walker," it said, "to ship from Sedalia to St. Louis en route to Kentucky the following blacks." The agent read the names carefully, then studied each of the slaves as if he was checking to see that the group standing before him agreed with the names on the certificate.

There was twenty-three-year-old John, the first slave that Walker had bought seven years earlier. John was muscled and strong legged from long days of hard work breaking hemp. The certificate also identified Emily and her five young children, all of them nearly asleep on their feet now. Next was Rachel and her two young children, also half-asleep. Anna and Patey were teenage girls old enough to work. Finally, the certificate listed twenty-three-year-old Billy. The certificate did not explain how they might all have been related. And if the slaves had surnames, they were not transcribed. They were property, no more entitled to a surname than a hay rake or a mule.

The station agent only glanced at the certificate, then handed it back to Walker. He could not permit Walker and his slaves to board the train, he said.

Walker was confused. Did the agent think there was a discrepancy between the list and the group Walker had brought for shipment?

No, the agent explained. The Pacific Railroad had several lawsuits pending against it for slave transport. One of the company's officials had complained that if they were held liable for slave transport, the railroad would soon be bankrupt. The agent told Walker that the transport of slaves was a risk the railroad was no longer willing to take.

Walker protested. The certificate was signed by local military officials. Walker invited the agent to walk the block to the Sedalia encampment to check for himself if he wanted.

There was no need, the agent said. A squad of Union troops stationed in Sedalia would arrive momentarily for the day's duty guarding the depot. But regardless of what the troops said, the station agent explained, Walker and his slaves would *not* be allowed to board the train.

The squad of soldiers, bearing their weapons, arrived in a matter of minutes. Walker again presented his certificate to the soldiers. They did not even bother to look at it. They explained that they were under standing orders not to permit the shipment of slaves to another state. That was the end of it.

Walker pressed them to explain why the young provost marshal had issued them a permit in the first place.

They said he must not have seen the recent order against shipment.

But, Walker objected, the permission he had just received obviously countermanded any such order.

The soldiers didn't care. They had *their* orders, and they intended to follow them.

Walker protested further. What was he supposed to do?

They told him that as far as they were concerned, he could get in his wagon and take his slaves back to his farm and put them to work again. But on no account was he going to take them to another state on a Pacific Railroad train.

There was another possible motive for the resolve of the soldiers. Only weeks before Walker's arrival at the platform, a bothersome peddler had come into the Sedalia encampment of soldiers crying, "Pins, thread, combs, buttons!" An Irish private ordered the peddler out of camp. "I've been ordered about for the last six months," the private had explained. "I've never had the pleasure of ordering another man."

The station soldiers, who also now had a chance to

deliver orders instead of receive them, made a line between Walker's group and the passenger cars. Walker had no choice then but to gather his slaves together again, climb back into his farm wagon, and disappear.

They had gone only a few hundred yards into the darkness, when Walker stopped the wagon and turned to his slaves. He was *not* going to return them to his farm, he said. He brandished his permit. Those thirteen slaves who were huddled in the wagon represented a good part of the nearly fifty thousand dollars of equity in land and slave "property" that he and his father had accumulated over the years through farming. He was not about to lose it all because some young Union soldiers half his age intended to follow orders.

The train was scheduled to depart the Sedalia station at approximately eight o'clock. Heading east, it would make its first stop to board passengers in Smithton, just a few miles down the track. For a short time, Smithton had been the terminus of the Pacific Railroad line, and the town had sprung up like a prairie flower. When the line was extended to its new terminus in Sedalia, the once radiant flower of Smithton quickly wilted. All that was left of the town was a boarding platform, a water tank, and a few buildings. There were no Union soldiers camped nearby. Walker and his brother could gallop the wagon team to Smithton. They could be there before sunup. When the train arrived from Sedalia to board more passengers, he could board it with his slaves and be on his way. The Union forces in Sedalia would be none the wiser.

Walker's intention to board the train in Smithton made escape a possibility for his slaves. Smithton had become nearly a ghost town. There were few inhabitants. There was no Main Street with businesses preparing to open for the day. There were no livery stables or open cattle yards that escapees would have to negotiate before they could disappear into nearby thick woods. If just one of them could escape and go for help, Walker would not be able to leave the rest of the slaves unguarded while he ran down the lone fugitive.

Walker and his brother drove the team of horses at a gallop along a frontier trail from Sedalia to Smithton. The sky had turned gray from the approaching sunrise when they arrived at the Smithton station. Walker said goodbye to his brother, who departed in the wagon. Then he herded his thirteen slaves toward the platform.

John waited and watched as one-by-one his family and fellow slaves stepped up onto the platform. He had looked for an opportunity to escape on the wagon ride from Sedalia to Smithton. But with Walker's brother on hand to guard the party of slaves, Walker was free to pursue any of them who tried to escape, and the opportunity for John to make a run for it had passed.

Walker stood calmly on the platform, as if he felt there would be no more surprises ahead of him. After all, he knew his own slaves. They worked hard and had always been compliant. In the gray stillness, there was nothing to suggest the furor of escape, nothing to make Walker tense or wary.

Once his family had all gathered beside Walker, John didn't hesitate. There were no soldiers or a platform agent to stop him now. The railroad right-of-way ditch promised some concealment. If he could get to it quickly, he could make a safe getaway.

John bolted for the ditch. It took Walker a moment to wake up to what was happening. Walker shouted, fired his pistol, and leaped off the platform as if he would take up the chase. Then he stopped and looked at the group of remaining slaves. They were a significant equity. There was no point in risking the loss of that valuable equity in pursuit of a lone fugitive. Still gripping his pistol, he jumped back up on the platform and waited for the train.

John headed back for Sedalia at a brisk run, splashing through creek beds, skirting patches of open prairie, and keeping to thick woods of oak, hickory, and walnut.

He moved as swiftly and as quietly as he could, fearful that even the snap of a dead twig would betray his presence to the bushwhackers and guerillas in the area. If they captured him, they would be just as ruthless as the mob who a few years before had dragged a slave accused of murder and rape from jail in Georgetown, just north of Sedalia. On the steps of the Georgetown courthouse, the mob had put the fate of the accused slave in the hands of the local citizenry: should the slave be lynched or burned alive? The decision was to burn him alive, and he had been taken to the outskirts of town and tied by wrist chains to a walnut sapling. All the slaves from the surrounding farms were made to watch in horror as he was set on fire and then pleaded for his life as the flames engulfed him.

To those slaves who watched him burn and to those who subsequently heard about the incident, it was not the object lesson it was meant to be on the inevitability of white man's justice. Instead, it was an object lesson on white cruelty. But for John the chances of being lynched or burned alive as a fugitive seemed a risk worth taking if he could rescue his own family. Once he got back to Sedalia, he could alert the soldiers who had refused to let Walker on the train. They had seemed to be sympathetic to the plight of the slaves. They surely would be incensed to learn that Walker had defied them. They would know exactly what to do to come to the rescue.

At a brisk run still, John reached Sedalia and passed the livery stables, then the Overland Stage offices, which were beginning to stir now with preparation for the new day. Dawn was just breaking behind him when he reached the platform of the Ives Hotel and found the same soldiers still there, guarding the platform like watchful loiterers.

The Pacific Railroad train was beginning to load passengers when John leaped onto the platform and confronted the soldiers. Mr. Walker had defied them, he explained. He had taken all the slaves to Smithton to board the train with them there. His wife and children were among the group. They would all be lost to him forever if the soldiers didn't rescue them.

The soldiers explained that they were under orders to guard the platform. They could not abandon their post. There was nothing they could do to help. They were as adamant about their orders to stay at their post as they had been to turn away Walker.

John was momentarily speechless. To be awakened in the middle of the night and told of Walker's plan had been heartbreaking. But hope for rescue had arisen when the soldiers on the platform stopped Walker. Those hopes had been dashed when Walker and his brother carted them all to Smithton. Then hope for all of them had again risen when John had bolted into the night. Now, for John those same hopes had been dashed a second time with the soldiers' explanation that they couldn't leave their posts.

What was he to do?

If he wanted his family and the others rescued, the solders explained, his best bet was to make a run for Otterville. After the train's brief stop in Smithton, it would move on to Otterville.

Otterville? John had never heard of Otterville.

There was a small cantonment of Union troops just east of Otterville, the soldiers said. Their duty was to guard a bridge over the Lamine River. Perhaps those soldiers could muster a rescue party and intercept the train.

The Lamine Bridge. John had never heard of that either.

Head straight east, the soldiers told him, into the sun that was just about to appear on the horizon. Follow the railroad tracks and the right-of-way. The route would take him straight through that hotbed of guerilla activity called Little Dixie. Stay out of sight of the bushwhackers, the soldiers warned. If he was spotted by bushwhackers, he was doomed.

Yes, he knew that.

Could he run?

Yes, he could run.

The train wasn't scheduled to depart the station in Sedalia for approximately an hour. He would have to get to Otterville and alert the troops at the Lamine Bridge before the train's scheduled arrival there at nine o'clock. The soldiers glanced at their watches. It was just after seven. He had almost two hours to run a little more than twenty miles to Otterville and the Lamine Bridge. He would have to run at a good clip. Could he do that? the soldiers asked him.

He could work hard from before sunrise until after dark. He could use his powerful arms all day long to cut and then break hemp. He could run from one corner of Walker's farm to the other, because walking wasted time and reflected indolence. But he wasn't sure he could run swiftly for twenty long miles.

He would have to, they said, if he wanted to rescue his family. There was no time to waste. He better get going.

# CHAPTER 3

# John

John leaped off the platform onto the train tracks and headed east. The streets of Sedalia were beginning to fill with citizens going to work in the stores along Main Street. The site of a Negro bolting down the middle of the street in the morning light would have suggested a runaway slave and drawn immediate pursuit, perhaps even gunfire. Slave catchers had had a field day preying on fugitive slaves. A chase party on horseback would be quickly formed to run him down. If they caught him, he faced the possibility of severe punishment. He might be whipped with cowhide, then have salt rubbed into the gashes. He might be tortured, then lynched. There were stories of captured runaways who had been castrated, had their ears cropped, or had their feet cut off.

He stayed on the railroad tracks until he found that trying to coordinate his stride with the intervals of the ties slowed him down. He left the tracks and scrambled into the right-of-way ditch. But sloshing through the occasional standing water in the ditch also slowed him down; and as soon as he had achieved the rolling hills and open prairie east of Sedalia, he came up out of the ditch.

His safest route to Otterville was through the woods and bushes. But the underbrush was so thick it would have slowed him to a crawl, and there was always the danger that he would surprise secret woods encampments of bushwhackers. So now he loped along the open fields abutting the woods, keeping the Pacific Railroad tracks always on his left in the distance.

Long hours of field labor every day on the Walker farm led him to believe that he had the stamina to keep going. While Rachel and Emily, their children at their sides, slaved as house servants for the Walker family, John and Billy worked in the fields, mainly breaking hemp. They called it a "nigger crop" because the work of extracting its fibers for rope manufacture was so dirty and exhausting that no white man would do it. The easy part was cutting it with sickles, shocking it, then spreading it out in the sun and leaving it to rot. Next came the hard work of breaking the hemp—lifting and pounding the stalks with a heavy wood brake until the mushy pith could be extracted from the stalks. Slaves were expected to break a hundred pounds of hemp a day, and there was a small incentive of a few extra pennies for exceeding the quota. "Wanted to hire," the ads for purchasing a slave sometimes said, "an industrious Negro man." For breaking hemp, only healthy and hardy slaves could do the work, and *man* was the key for slave owners seeking to purchase additional slaves.

It was ironic that years of such exhausting and slavish work might now be just the preparation John needed to escape it. But it was as if history was chasing him, as relentless and inescapable in its course as a pack of barking and howling hounds. No matter how fast he ran, what chance did he have of escaping the momentum of years of slavery? It wasn't just thick woods and deep ravines that he needed to negotiate to get to Otterville and the Lamine Bridge. It wasn't just bushwhackers he needed to elude. He was running to escape decades of history.

One of the hotbeds of slave history was the rich alluvial soils and open prairie that John was now running across. Missouri had wanted to enter the Union in 1819 as a slave state, but abolitionists argued that such a move would open the way to slavery in the North. The two sides quarreled over the issue, sometimes violently. Eventually, Congress tried to resolve the conflict by striking a compromise, permitting Missouri to enter the Union as a slave state but forbidding slavery in whatever states would be carved out of territories north of the Missouri border.

This compromise might have resolved the issue for Congress, but it did not resolve the issue in Missouri. For Missouri slaves, the idea that the state was a promontory jutting up into a sea of free territories and states invited escape and freedom. Slaveholders demanding the return of those fugitive slaves cited provisions of the Constitution requiring that fugitives "shall be delivered up on claim" to their owners. It was the law! The slave-catching business was "lawful and patriotic." Refuge states were required to deliver runaways back to their owners. If the Constitution wasn't enough justification for slave ownership, slaveholders argued that the institution of slavery was biblically sanctioned. Finally, to give still more authority to slave owners, in 1850 Congress passed the Fugitive Slave Law, ordering that all runaway slaves should be brought back to their masters. Abolitionists were nothing but "Negro thieves," those who favored slavery argued, and they formed vigilante groups to punish the "nigger stealers."

Slavery laws and biblical sanctions made the lives of slaves still worse. Just miles from where John ran for his life and the lives of his family, a female slave who clubbed to death the owner who had raped her was convicted of murder and hanged. For slaves it was one more indication of their condition as mere property and beasts of burden, who could be abused however their white masters chose. Abductions and escapes in Missouri increased tenfold. "Underground" escape routes from Missouri to Kansas, or even as far as Canada, were as well-worn as frontier trails. With Harriet Beecher Stowe's *Uncle Tom's Cabin*, a huge audience of readers wept at the images of the slave Eliza, carrying her baby and full of despair, leaping desperately from one ice flow to another to cross the frozen Ohio River to freedom.

The decline of slavery in Missouri prompted anxious slave owners to sell their slave property at any price or to ship them to Kentucky, where the institution of slavery appeared more durable. The continued fight between abolitionists and slavers in Missouri caused slave owners to refuge slaves to the Confederate interior. But some Union forces that made salients into rebel territory insisted that the slaves were "contraband" that could be confiscated and employed in Union army services "to which they may be best adapted." One Union general vowed, "I will never be voluntarily instrumental in returning a poor wretch to slavery." But slaveholders swore that, come what may, they would get their runaway property back.

Again, Congress stepped in to try to end the standoff. It was "no part of the duty of soldiers of the U.S.," they resolved, to capture and return fugitive slaves. Slave owners insisted the resolution flew in the face of the Constitution. The resolution also raised more issues than it settled. What was considered contraband? And how was the slave owner to prove that the confiscated property was his?

The federal government considered the bushwhackers and Southern sympathizers in Missouri to be no better than rebels. Couldn't the property of these disloyals be seized, even if slavery was legal in Missouri? Union generals proceeded to issue edicts that freed slaves whose Missouri masters were rebel sympathizers. The action infuriated Missouri slave owners like Walker. President Lincoln, eager to mollify Missouri slaveholders and keep Missouri in the Union, quickly stepped in to overrule his generals.

Union commanders and their troops were not authorized to interfere with the servants owned by peaceful citizens. "This is a war for the Union," Lincoln's secretary of war said. It was *not* a war to abolish slavery. All existing rights of loyal Union states, including slavery, were to be respected and maintained.

Lincoln's actions meant that fugitive slaves were denied safe harbor in military camps. But neither could the troops arrest them. If slaves came into Union encampments seeking freedom, they were to be turned away. But "discretion" was to be used in doing so.

The confusion worsened, and some generals ordered their troops to assist in recapturing runaways. Other generals argued that restoring slaves to their masters was tantamount to aiding and abetting the enemy. Furthermore, the slaves could serve as important sources of information on rebel troops. Meanwhile, the governor of Missouri complained that slaves were being held by Union armies against the wishes of their owners. But what if they were slaves who had been freed? And who was to determine if they were or weren't free?

The answer from military commanders was that the slaves were to be kept in army custody until civil authorities could decide the issue. Missouri commanders declared that their officers were to bar slave owners from searching for their runaways in military camps. "We are not nigger hunters," the commanders said. Government agents were expected to take over farms and plantations abandoned by owners fleeing to Confederate states. The abandoned slaves were to be supervised by Union agents until they could take care of themselves.

In Pettis County, Missouri—the site of Charles Walker's farm—the army's apparent hands-off policy for runaways created even more ambiguities. Missouri commanders issued permission certificates for some slaver owners to

ship their slaves to St. Louis. At the same time, other commanders refused to release two runaways to their owner.
The angry owner and his son then came into camp and
seized the two slaves. Two hundred Union troops immediately surrounded the owner and his son and began stoning them.

Elsewhere in Missouri, slaveholders were warned that
if they entered army ranks in an attempt to take back
their runaways, they would be shot. Emboldened by the
army's protection, slaves in custody of Union soldiers
went out armed to seize other slaves still in bondage.
Meanwhile, slave owners continued to demand that they
be allowed to come into camps to search for their fugitive
slaves. In the face of so much chaos, one Union commander complained, "There is a screw loose somewhere."

For some Union generals it was all too confusing. What
should be done with those slaves *already* in their custody?
The unsatisfactory answer was that the slaves should not
have been permitted into camp in the first place. Slave
and master should be left to settle their affairs themselves. But this policy only continued the Union Army's
predicament. One commander complained, "I tell the
[masters] that I can use no force to aid them in recovering
their Negroes." At the same time, the commander complained, he could do nothing to stop the owners if they
came into camp.

With the soldiers looking the other way, some slave
owners broke into Union camps and seized their slaves,
then held them in chains in swamps, where they waited
to be shipped south. But escape continued to be a risk,
and eventually some slave owners branded their slaves on
the forehead to prevent additional escapes.

In January of 1863 John was laboring in the fields of his
master, Charles Walker, when news of Abraham Lincoln's

Emancipation Proclamation arrived. The proclamation promised freedom only to the slaves of those secessionist states that refused to return to the Union. Missouri, which had not seceded, was not included in the proclamation, and Lincoln's announcement meant little or nothing to John and other Northern slaves.

Loyal slave owners in the North complained to Lincoln that runaways left them without labor to work their farms. Crops were rotting for want of harvest labor. If the owners couldn't enter Union camps and if they could expect no help from Union soldiers, how were they to get their slaves back? The answer seemed to be to sell the slaves, as Charles Walker was trying to do, before they became worthless or ran away. Kentucky became a haven for slave owners trying to sell their property, either to other slavers or to Union armies seeking laborers. Slaves were sold at auction on the steps of the Louisville courthouse. Kentucky, which was where John's family was headed on the Pacific Railroad train, became the nation's "slave mart," with "slave pens" holding slaves until they could be sold. Missouri runaways were kept in jails in St. Louis until they could be shipped to Kentucky.

The confusion and ambiguity seemed to promise John little hope. If or when he reached those Union troops guarding the Lamine Bridge, would he be given safe harbor or turned away? Would he be put back on the train with Walker's other slaves? Or would the train be stopped and the slaves on it let go? Would he and his family become fugitives on a trail to freedom or be penned up while waiting to be sold like cattle?

Despite those uncertainties, John ran at full speed, cutting now and then through the high prairie grass. He slid down the embankment of timbered ravines and creek beds, then scrambled up out of the ravines, his legs numb from the ice cold water. He slowed his pace only to cautiously crest rolling hills, fearful that he would surprise bushwhackers out of sight on the back slopes. He kept his course straight east into the sunrise, changing it only periodically to circle the edges of swamps and ponds.

He ran with confidence. His legs felt strong. He was breathing evenly and steadily. There was no cold wind for him to buck. Dry leaves from the stands of oak, hickory, elm, and walnut crackled under his feet. The occasional busy squirrels that he passed hardly seemed to notice him. Birdsong filled the air. The morning suggested a world of order and peace and promise.

John was making a desperate run, not just for *his* life, but for the lives of his family. And the prospects for the success of John's run seemed to be increasing by the minute. His legs still felt strong. They moved in long, quick strides without effort or thought. The only thing that occupied his mind was how he would make a convincing and desperate plea for help once he reached the Lamine Bridge.

He was still moving fast when the fatigue suddenly hit him. He felt like he was breathing fire, and his legs turned heavy. He tried to keep a straight course, but he staggered and wove as if each footfall had a tired will of its own. His face burned. Hot sweat stung his eyes. His shoulders ached. He could hardly raise and pump those same strong arms with which he had broken hemp.

Why hadn't he prepared for this? Why hadn't he sprinted from one end of Walker's farm to the other, building strength and stamina? But how could he have known that he would one day need to make an exhausting run for freedom? How could he have known what a superhuman effort it would take?

A short rest would have given him strength to resume running at an even faster pace. But he fought the temptation to stop and walk. What if the train overtook him because he had stopped to rest? His desperate run would have been made in vain. His family would come and go at the Otterville station without rescue. Who knew where they would wind up? He would never see them again. And they were his one refuge in a sea of misery.

# CHAPTER 4
## Sergeant Francis Merchant

John passed the Otterville station without slowing his pace. There was a small group of townspeople standing on the station platform. Half of them had no intention of boarding the train. They were there only because the noisy arrival of the morning train promised the only excitement of what would otherwise be a sleepy day in the village.

Otterville had been first settled in the middle of what had been described as a "howling wilderness." In the 1850s, in an effort to avoid the obscurity of a rural hamlet, the planners who laid out the streets put a town square at the center of the village. That town square was soon surrounded by houses, a few meeting lodges, business establishments, and a brick storehouse.

One mile east of Otterville, the Lamine River snaked its way toward the Missouri River. At a site where cattlemen had once driven their herds across sandbars of the river, the Pacific Railroad constructed a trestle bridge that was part of their project to extend their railway line west from St. Louis. The bridge was a crude crosshatch of timbers of the same kind that President Lincoln had once described as "nothing but beanpoles and cornstalks."

The Lamine Bridge may have looked flimsy and dangerous, but with its completion Otterville became the temporary terminus of the Pacific Railroad line. And the town prospered like a "green bay tree." A large hotel was built near the Otterville depot to serve the train passengers. But with the extension of the railway west from Otterville in 1861, Sedalia became the new terminus and "rose like magic" from the prairie. The hotel in Otterville was moved to Sedalia. The village that had tried to escape obscurity sank back into it. Eventually, the grandest buildings of Otterville would stand only as a reminder of the perishable character of life.

Cooper County, in which Otterville was located, comprised that part of Missouri known as Little Dixie, because of the concentration of Southerners who had settled there with slaves to work the fertile bottomlands of the nearby Missouri River. In the election of 1860, only twenty people of some thirteen thousand residents in Cooper County voted for Abraham Lincoln. Those who voted for him had their names published in newspapers as "items of curiosity." With the start of the Civil War, Otterville was temporarily crowded with immigrants fleeing the chaos and destruction of other parts of Missouri. They were cold and hungry. But there was no shelter or food for them, and they were soon in danger of starving. The Union command in the area appealed to Washington for rations that would get the immigrants through the winter. Meanwhile, the war policies of the Lincoln administration were blamed for the chaos.

Those policies meant that the village of Otterville and its surrounding countryside began to develop secession convictions. One soldier described the area as a secession district. Another soldier noted in a letter to a friend that "secesh ladies" came into town dressed in fancy silks and furs. Otterville was a little-known spot on the map, but the Pacific Railroad line from St. Louis to Sedalia became a critical corridor for the transit of Union supplies and troops. And the high command of the Union felt that

Otterville and the surrounding region would be one of the focal points of the war in the West.

A company of German Home Guard militia from Missouri was sent to Otterville to guard the Lamine Bridge. They were strong Unionists and often characterized by their critics as "nigger lovers." Meanwhile, they were hardly the seasoned soldiers necessary for the protection of strategic ground. More soldiers, trained and experienced, were necessary. And in October of 1861 President Lincoln wrote to the commander of federal troops in Missouri that they were to guard the railroads and keep the supply lines open. "Employ as many men as you need," Lincoln said.

Union engineers went to work immediately to create defensive fortifications around the trestle bridge over the Lamine River. The typical defense for a railroad bridge was a sturdy but small blockhouse at one end of the bridge. But with the expectations by Union command that Otterville and the Lamine Bridge would be a critical battle site, the engineers dug two deep trenches, each a quarter mile long, that would give cover to five hundred Union soldiers in the event an attack came from rebel forces moving up from Arkansas.

As soon as the initial trenches were dug, a cantonment of federal troops was established on the bottomland alongside the river and beneath the bridge. In bitter winter cold, the ground as hard as cement, the soldiers labored to lengthen the trenches to accommodate a still larger force of defenders. It was slow, difficult work, and thirty-four soldiers died during the effort. But by mid-January of 1862 the expanded trenches were finally finished, and three thousand Union troops were ready for any attackers.

Piercing winds and the dampness of a Missouri winter, to troops, seemed more of a threat than rebel invaders, and the soldiers put up tents with stoves or built log huts with wood floors laid from packing boxes to protect against the ground cold. Meanwhile, rebel commanders making sorties into Missouri began destroying all railroad bridges and telegraph wires in their path. Blowing up bridges, however, required kegs of powder explosives, which had to be transported by mules. The easiest course was to make surprise attacks on bridges and set them on fire. "Look out for bridge burners," Union generals warned. "Shoot down everyone making the attempt."

While the war raged elsewhere, months passed with no threats to the bridge from Missouri bushwhackers. Then rebel guerillas threatened to sack the town of Boonville, just a few miles northeast on the Missouri River. The Union practice of scattering small forces across the area, like at the Lamine Bridge, was clearly a fatal policy, because it prevented the massing of troops for a coordinated offensive. So with Boonville in peril, all but a few of the Lamine Bridge guardians were moved to the threatened town to repel the enemy.

The trench fortifications protecting the Lamine Bridge were abandoned. Only one small detachment of twenty-eight Union soldiers was left to guard the bridge from inside a solid blockhouse. Despite the bridge's inconspicuous location, it was too important to lose, Union generals felt. "Save it!" they ordered, and the small force huddled in the blockhouse, ready for any attack.

On the night of October 9, 1863, a rebel cavalry unit of one hundred men, whose bloody hit-and-run tactics had already made the "waters of the Lamine run red," attacked the bridge. They approached from the surrounding woods, shouting wildly. The Union troops panicked, and it was a bloody but brief fight. Seventeen Union soldiers surrendered to the attackers, who quickly exchanged clothes with their prisoners and broke the Union soldiers' arms before releasing them. Finally, the guerillas burned the blockhouse, the huts, and the tents. They set fire to the crosshatch of bridge timbers and watched from the Lamine bottomland as the timbers fell "in a mass of seething, hissing fire" into the river. Once the fire was out, the guerillas gathered their horses and left without the loss of a single man.

After guerillas burned the bridge over the Lamine River, it did not take long for Union engineers to rebuild it, despite two snow storms that struck the area in October and November of 1863. The new bridge had no rail guards and was just a thin strip of railroad track anchored to stone piers and stretched for 160 yards across the river. But the line remained a critical transportation corridor for the Union Army, and commanders in St. Louis were determined to make sure the bridge wasn't burned again. To protect it they knew they would need a larger and stronger force than the small detachment of troops the rebels had quickly routed.

The Union turned to Colonel Alexander Wilkin, the commander of the Ninth Minnesota Volunteer Infantry Regiment. Wilkin was a tiny man, weighing hardly a hundred pounds and only five feet tall. Despite his size, Wilkin was a demanding and pugnacious military leader. He had shot and killed a fellow officer in a duel; and once while bringing his sword into position, he had accidentally struck another soldier in the face. He had served with distinction as an officer in the Mexican War under Zachary Taylor and had been part of the ferocious fight at the First Battle of Bull Run. After that battle, the governor of Minnesota appointed Wilkin to command the Ninth Regiment just formed in Minnesota. He was a forty-one-year-old bachelor who had dedicated his life to soldiering. After his appointment, he pledged to make the Ninth "the crack regiment of the state."

For weeks, while his regiment drilled in Jefferson City, Missouri, and waited to be sent into action, Wilkin had pestered his superiors about getting into the Civil War fight. His regiment had been formed over a year ago. His men were well trained, he argued. Despite the snow and the cold in Jefferson City, there had not been a single desertion from his regiment. Considering that 200,000 Union troops had already deserted in the course of the Civil War, the Ninth's record was an admirable one. Wilkin told his superiors that the men of his Minnesota regiment had grit and were ready to head south for the kind of epic action he had experienced at Bull Run.

Instead, on October 15, 1863, three hundred men and officers of Companies C and K of the Ninth Minnesota were ordered from Jefferson City to the Lamine River, to take up the humdrum duty of making sure the bridge wasn't burned again.

The men of Companies C and K of the Ninth Minnesota were frontier pioneers and settlers from southern Minnesota. Most of them had moved to the region after hearing that the land was so fecund that they could shoot deer and elk from the doors of their log cabins. With the removal of Indians from the land, settlers poured into Minnesota. They came through swamps and rivers and deep ravines and steep hills, expecting to find the Garden of Eden.

Instead, they found wolves, rattlesnakes, and long cold winters that turned the landscape into a white desert. Some lost their way in blizzards, freezing upright in snowdrifts. In the summers, they drowned, were struck by lightning, fell into well shafts, or were cut in half by sharp plow wheels. Kerosene lamps exploded and killed entire families. Others died of consumption, diphtheria, typhoid, croup, and broken hearts. Children died frequently, with the only explanation being "God took the child." The tragedies gave the settlers a crust as hard as turtle shell that protected a tender hope and a deep faith in God.

Still, candlelit shanties described as a "higher order of wigwam" soon dotted what had been empty prairie. Log houses with hay and sod roofs sheltered as many as two dozen settlers. Others simply dug holes in the ground and lived like prairie dogs. The women planted and dug potatoes and cooked slapjacks. The men planted wheat and then ground it with crude tin graters. They seeded the plowed fields with corn. They raised pigs and cattle and tried to make breachy horses obey their commands. They bought nails by the keg. They bought tin plates, grass scythes, pitchforks, hoes, grindstones, handsaws, paint.

In Mower County in southern Minnesota one of the first structures erected in the new prairie town of Austin was called the Great Barn. Built to serve as a general store as well as a place for worship and patriotic meetings, it was in the center of town along a Main Street still not cleared of hazel brush.

It may have seemed strange that earthbound, sod-busting, nail-driving farmers and their families could harbor any lofty convictions. But ardent patriotism had always been a characteristic of the settlers in Mower County. Once at an Independence Day celebration in the Great Barn, the main speaker of the evening had invoked the spirit of 1776; but in the patriotic fervor of the evening, he read from the Constitution instead of the Declaration of Independence.

Immediately after the firing on Fort Sumter in April of 1861, Minnesota offered to raise a regiment of a thousand men to fight the South. Lincoln was able to raise a force of 700,000 Union men. But by the spring of 1862, the war fever had subsided. War Department officials instructed the governors of each state to begin raising new volunteer regiments. The goal was 300,000 men.

The governors encouraged eligible men in each state to join the fight for the "old flag." The enemy was at the threshold of their homes. "Come one, come all," newspaper editorials urged, "who are able to bear arms."

The War Department established volunteer quotas for each state, based on population. The men would serve for three years, possibly less. Three years seemed an eternity, and volunteers came forward slowly. In the face of the reluctance, on July 16, 1862, Congress resorted to compulsory service through conscription into state militias and passed the Federal Militia Act. The next day, Lincoln signed the bill putting all able-bodied men from eighteen to forty-five under the threat of compulsory service.

Lincoln recalled from his days in Illinois that state militias as an effective fighting force had been laughed at. Their officers, Lincoln said, carried pinewood swords "about nine feet long" and wore pasteboard cocked hats. But under the provisions of the Militia Act of 1862, those soldiers who were drafted would make up for any shortages in volunteer quotas. Meanwhile, Lincoln had the authority to call those state militia units into federal service for a period as long as nine months.

To minimize the appearance of federal government interference, states took control of the conscription process. County assessors, despite criticism of favoritism, drew up the enrollment lists of eligible men, whose names went into a cardboard box or a rotation device called a "jury wheel." The names were drawn by a man with a blindfold.

The process seemed no better than a roll of the dice. Meanwhile, the men who chose to volunteer rather than wait to have their names drawn would receive a one-hundred-dollar federal bounty, twenty-five of it payable upon signing up. Even if volunteering meant three years, the signing bounties were attractive. Newspapers explained the choices succinctly: "Volunteer and receive bounties, or wait to be drafted and get nothing." Thousands now offered themselves as volunteers for the federal army.

In Minnesota, broadsides and county newspapers announced, "Patriotic Mass Meeting. Let patriotic inhabitants everywhere be present." The governor of Minnesota insisted that all else was insignificant "beneath the shadow of the stupendous national calamity" of the Civil War. Mower County officials offered five bushels of wheat for each volunteer's family, and some Mower County citizens offered a cash supplement to the federal bounty.

The threat of being drafted and the bounties may have done more to prompt volunteers than patriotism. Also, up and down the Minnesota River settlers were fleeing Dakota Indians angry over the failure of the federal government to make annual annuity payments due them for the sale of their ancestral lands. White traders had no sympathy and told the starving Indians that they could eat grass to satisfy their hunger.

Indian rage over the white man's long-standing deceit and neglect exploded, and hundreds of prairie settlers were killed. The Indians laid siege to prairie villages not far from Austin. Hastily assembled militia men with muskets and pitchforks manned barricades to drive off the attackers. In Austin they posted sentinels who were instructed to fire three shots to warn the citizens if they were under Indian attack. One terrified French immigrant grabbed a rifle and his diary and tried to take refuge in a hollow oak tree. But he slipped deeper into the tree's hollow. "Can not get out," he wrote in his diary. "Surely must die." Woodchoppers did not find his bones and his diary until half a century later. It was a horror as distant as Egyptian history, but his mummified remains stood as a grisly reminder of how powerful that Indian fear in Minnesota had been.

As the news of the Dakota uprising spread, Mower County settlers packed the Great Barn in Austin for their own "Patriotic Mass Meeting." Citizens from all over Mower County responded; among them were farm wives in crinoline woven from grapevines and barefoot women in Shaker bonnets who waved white handkerchiefs. A young Union lieutenant from St. Paul asked, "Who does not burn with a desire to rush forth to rescue the Union"— from wild Indians, he meant, as well as from hellish rebels. "Men of Mower County," the young lieutenant implored his audience, "away to the emergency of the time!"

The men responded with "hurrahs" and signed up to serve. With hundreds of Minnesota farmsteads on fire and settlers fleeing for their lives, a Civil War a thousand miles away to determine the fate of Negro slaves seemed less important than saving the state, and especially Mower County, from being overwhelmed by Indians.

Hundreds of men enlisted. They were as young as eighteen and as old as their fifties, from every farm and village and township in Mower County. One of the first to volunteer was twenty-one-year-old Francis Merchant. In 1849 he had emigrated with his parents and his sister from France to the United States. The family had settled briefly in New York; but in search of frontier opportunity, they moved to Wisconsin. When news reached them that there was cheap, fertile land available in southern Minnesota, they were among the first rush of settlers. They homesteaded a quarter section of farmland just beyond the western edge of Mower County. The prairie land was flat as the ocean, with no nearby lakes, rivers, creeks, or even a slough. But they dug a deep well, and each spring and summer the sky darkened and then cracked with lightning bolts before the rain came like it was being pitched from a heavenly wash basin. The land produced head-high grasses and a "perfect paradise of flowers."

They built a claim shanty, then a one-room log cabin just eighteen-by-eighteen feet for the family of four. For flooring, they split wood slabs from logs and then smoothed them with a broadax. By this time, Francis's father was fifty and beginning to slow down from the hard labor of farming, so it was young Francis who took over the farm chores. He planted cottonwood trees, whose white seeds drifted to the ground like snowflakes each spring. He planted a grove of ash and maple and oak, to break the force of the fierce winter winds. At sixteen years old he cut the six-foot prairie grasses with a heavy scythe that at first he could hardly lift and swing. At eighteen he could sweat and labor all day long behind a horse-drawn sickle bar that cut grain. By the time he was twenty he had grown to nearly six feet, with a handsome dark complexion and hard gray eyes that made him look older than he was. He exuded experience and confidence, even though there were men twice his age among the volunteers. *Mer*-shaunt it was pronounced, giving him another distinction among the volunteers with sharp names like Felch and Pratt and Pye. Francis Merchant's superiors immediately made him a sergeant.

For some of the soldiers, the patriotism of the moment had battled against their reluctance to leave behind their families and farms in order to fight in a far-off war to preserve the Union and obtain freedom for the Negro. Not a single black man lived in Mower County. A hunting party from St. Paul had once come through the county with a Negro slave named Dred Scott. Then two Negro fugitives from Missouri had passed through Austin on their way to Canada and freedom. They were described as "fine looking fellows." But they could have been aliens from another planet. Now, the young, sturdy farm boys of Mower County were expected to go fight in Virginia or Mississippi, while their own state was burning.

# CHAPTER 5

# Private Henry Ehmke

While Mower County held war meetings and volunteers signed up for duty, less than eighty miles away as the crow flies or as settlers traveled on horseback lay the Mississippi River town of Winona, Minnesota. There, a twenty-one-year-old German immigrant named Henry Ehmke had been following the Civil War news carefully. He was a tall, lop-eared string bean with a bony face that would have passed for the skull of a dead man if it hadn't been for a bristly mustache with points as sharp as splitting wedges.

He had been drawn to Winona by the excitement of a boisterous river town that had sprung up on a sandbar nestled up against the limestone bluffs of the river. Across the river in Wisconsin there were more bluffs like the busts of sentinels with slope shoulders and tiny limestone faces peeking out from green beards of scrub oak.

The town's namesake was an Indian woman named Wenona, who, legend claimed, had jumped from one of those limestone bluffs to her death after her father forbid her to marry the man she loved. But Winona didn't mean death. Winona meant muddy streets with busy citizens and the acrid smell of burning sawdust that served as fuel for the flour mills. Winona meant steamboat whistles and calliopes and crowds waving handkerchiefs from the public levee to greet the riverboats delivering lumber and wheat. Winona meant *life*.

Those immigrants like Henry Ehmke who had poured into bustling Winona found work in one of the town's many saw mills, cutting shingles and pickets for $1.50 a day, six days a week. While the rich lumber barons and milling moguls of the town built Victorian houses with turrets and stone porches, the mill workers lived in tents or boarding houses. Sunday mornings, they went to church, then read newspapers in the language of their homeland.

Henry Ehmke's English was, at first, broken and uncertain, but he learned the new language quickly. Sunday afternoons, he walked to the levee to join the crowds that gathered to watch the paddle wheelers arrive. The turning paddlewheels, the oxcarts creaking along Main Street day and night, the river sliding slowly along without pause—*everything* in Winona was in motion and nothing stood still. What wasn't moving—bags of wheat stacked on the levee—was only cargo *waiting* to be shipped downriver.

Winona was the third largest city in Minnesota, but it seemed as transitory and impermanent as the sandbar on which it had been built. The river town served as a jumping off point for settlers, their last opportunity to buy livestock and food supplies before heading for the plains and homestead opportunities. "Boots, Shoes," one Main Street storefront sign read, as if to encourage folks to move along.

Winona seemed to be just a way station along the road to something else, something "weightier than local chemistries." Just what that might be, Henry Ehmke had not been sure. Then the German-language newspapers he read began to carry the Civil War news with calls for volunteers to fight. "Secesh rabble" were killing German Union men, and the families of the dead soldiers gave "piteous cries" for their dead loved ones. "How long will

Germans continue to be murdered?" the editors asked. "Does not the blood of the murdered demand energetic action at last?"

Henry Ehmke read with interest that Winona would form a full company of men. They would be mostly Germans but also Poles and Italians and Frenchmen, and they would fight side by side. The company would be part of the Ninth Regiment Minnesota Volunteer Infantry, with soldiers from Austin and Winona and nearly a dozen other small towns and villages in Minnesota. Ehmke wasted no time in enlisting.

Cheering crowds gathered in Winona and on Main Street in Austin to see the men march off to be mustered in St. Paul. They were such an impressive spectacle of sturdiness and bravery that the newspapers predicted they would form a "solid column of bayonets and cannon, from the Atlantic to the Mississippi." They would drive the rebels into the gulf "like frightened sheep." The men were presented with a flag sewn by "loving hands." Even more inflamed with patriotism now, they promised to "bring it back, or fall with it."

In St. Paul they held an official "mustering day" in August of 1862 to determine which of the volunteers hadn't already deserted or died and were still alive and ready to fight. Then they formed companies for the new regiment. Military bands played. Again, citizens and families lined the parade grounds. Officers in full military dress, their brass buttons blinking in the sun, watched as the green volunteers assembled. The men signed an oath of allegiance and pledged to serve for three years. Physicians gave them a superficial exam to weed out the aged, the infirm, the blind, and the deaf.

The new soldiers from Winona and Mower County were organized into the Ninth Minnesota Volunteer Infantry Regiment. They were told they would be assigned garrison duty against those marauding Indians on the Minnesota frontier, liberating experienced soldiers to fight in the Civil War. St. Paul editors wrote, "Who would not gladly have the honor of serving . . . in this glorious crusade?"

The regiment's first duty, in the late summer of 1862, was to protect Minnesota's frontier settlers from warring Indians. Then the Ninth Regiment moved to St. Peter, Minnesota, where Colonel Wilkin put his troops through daily close-order drilling and marching. Meanwhile, Wilkin remained demanding and pugnacious and complained to his commanders in St. Paul that there was no forage in the area for his troops or his animals. The regiment's horses were broken down and useless. His officers were inexperienced and had "difficulty in attending to the necessary duties of their post." There were no mess kits. Knives, forks, spoons had to be furnished by the men. "We have no blankets," he said. His men couldn't drill, and their ragged uniforms made them look more like a ragtag posse than a disciplined regiment of Union troops.

From St. Peter the regiment moved to Mankato to keep order among the citizens during the mass hanging of thirty-eight Dakota Indians who had participated in the uprising.

Despite his regiment's inexperience and equipment shortages, Colonel Wilkin vowed that the regiment would shoot down disorderly citizens without hesitation. But the huge crowd fell silent when the thirty-eight prisoners dropped at once from noose ropes fixed to a square scaffold. The sight of the prisoners twisting and thrashing in the air as they died served as a stark lesson to the men of the Ninth on the agony and certainty of wartime justice.

By April of 1863 the Ninth Regiment found itself posted at Fort Ridgely in western Minnesota on a promontory above the Minnesota River. With each new assignment for the regiment, Wilkin grew even more pugnacious. Again he wrote to his commanders in St. Paul, this time to complain that his subordinates, some of whom were over a foot taller than he was, were making disrespectful remarks about their feisty little leader. He was in a continual battle with his officers, who were only interested in payday.

In September the regiment received marching orders to ship by steamboat from Winona to Dixie. In preparation, Colonel Wilkin drilled the men daily on formation marching: "Forward!" "Left!" "Right!" "Left oblique!" "Right oblique!" It was exhausting and tedious and seemed to the soldiers to have nothing whatsoever to do with enabling one man to shoot a fellow countryman on a smoky battlefield.

Before the regiment left, they were enrolled into the Union Army as federal soldiers. To replace their ragged dress, they were issued frock coats and forage caps. They took an oath to defend the Constitution of the United States against all enemies foreign and domestic. They swore that with the help of God they would faithfully discharge the duties of the office on which they were about to enter. They were read the Articles of War and the penalties for violation, one of which was death as abrupt and agonizing as the fate of those Indians who had been hanged in Mankato.

They were given two weeks leave to visit their families and homes before they departed for Civil War battlefields. In Winona the new recruits, including the raw-boned Private Ehmke, strutted down Main Street in their new Union uniforms as if they were generals. In Austin the citizens of Mower County served Francis Merchant and others from his company a sumptuous meal at one of the new two-story hotels. The soldiers were treated to barrels of apples, and they danced until early morning before returning to duty.

Their wives and family and girlfriends kissed them goodbye the next morning when they boarded a steamboat in Winona. A crowd waving handkerchiefs saw them off from the levee as they boarded the sternwheeler *Chippewa Falls*. "Write often!" their loved ones called to them as the steamboat pulled away. Farther down the Mississippi in La Crosse, Wisconsin, where more crowds lined up, waving flags and handkerchiefs and cheering wildly, they boarded a train for Chicago.

The nearly one thousand soldiers of the Ninth Minnesota Volunteer Infantry thought they were headed for Vicksburg or Chattanooga. Instead, they headed for St. Louis, where bushwhackers and Confederate guerillas were wreaking havoc. They arrived in St. Louis the morning of October 12, 1863. The red clover was in bloom when they were lodged in Benton Barracks, where after four days of travel by steamboat and train and on foot, during which their battle anxieties mounted, they had their first good night's sleep.

But the next morning, they were on the move again, this time west to Jefferson City, the capitol of Missouri. In Jefferson City it was raining and cold, not the stinging, blowing cold of the Minnesota prairie, but something almost worse, a soggy, heavy chill that soaked deep into the bones. The men tried to keep warm by foraging fence rail and then burning it in the makeshift stoves of their conical Sibley tents. This did not reflect the toughness or discipline of properly trained troops, Colonel Wilkin felt, and he ordered the men to stop foraging for firewood. But the cold soldiers could be as combative as Wilkin. They reacted with understandable anger and secretly laid clumps of sod over the stovepipe of Wilkin's roomy wall tent. He stumbled out of his warm but smoky tent choking and gasping and promptly reversed his order.

Bridge burning and destruction by rebel forces had become a regular occurrence along several Missouri railroad lines. Small detachments of Union troops were assigned to guard the bridges. One of those detachments was comprised of the men from Companies C and K of the Ninth Minnesota. Approximately two hundred from the two companies left Jefferson City by train to take up the monotonous duty of guarding the Lamine Bridge along the Pacific Railroad line running from Sedalia to Jefferson City to St. Louis.

Thirty-five-year-old Captain David Wellman of Winona, Minnesota, commanded the detachment. He was an experienced engineer whose expertise was bridge building. If the rebels damaged the bridge again, Wellman had the experience to repair it. But Wellman had left behind a prosperous engineering business that stretched from Minnesota to Indiana. Reluctant to abandon that business, he had not been swept up in the initial wave of enlistment excitement in Winona. But the call to fight for the preservation of the Union had been too strong to resist, and he eventually volunteered. He had been immediately appointed to the rank of lieutenant in the Ninth Minnesota; but in a matter of days, on the strength of a dignified, scholarly bearing that made him stand out among the plowmen and mill workers of Winona, he found himself promoted to first lieutenant, then captain with a company to run.

Wellman had been the sole support for his aging parents in Winona, and as soon as the regiment moved from Minnesota to Missouri, he wrote his commanders to explain that he had "abandoned" his business to serve the country. Since his enlistment, he said, he had not had a single day to devote to the settlement of his business affairs. If his mind wasn't on his military duties, it was because he had pressing obligations elsewhere.

For Captain David Wellman the Lamine Bridge duty offered an opportunity to get away from the hustle and bustle of regimental headquarters in Jefferson City and tend to his business affairs.

Meanwhile, he petitioned his superiors in Jefferson City, asking for a leave of absence so that he could return to Minnesota and properly oversee those affairs. He also worried about his parents. How would they hold up if it proved to be another ferocious Minnesota winter? He had in his company dependable junior officers and noncoms, he said, and among them was Sergeant Francis Merchant, who would assume the day-to-day duties of running his company while he was on leave. While Captain Wellman waited to hear whether or not his request for a leave had been approved, he could do little else about his business affairs except to try to handle them by mail.

For Sergeant Merchant the Lamine cantonment was a place where he was determined to exercise the same dog-gedness with which he had carved a productive farm out of the Minnesota prairie. For Henry Ehmke, the restless string bean private, the cantonment was just another way station in his peripatetic life.

For days, the Lamine Bridge detachment did nothing but assemble for roll call, dig latrines, stand inspection, and then drill, drill, drill. It snowed regularly. The men grew beards to keep the cold and grit out of their lungs. They stood boring watches in the blockhouse. They complained that the food was inedible, joking that the bread was so unchewable that it could have been used to make cannonball-resistant tents. Their officers read them the Articles of War every Sunday. Among those articles were the regulations against and the penalties for mutiny. For the men, the conclusion was clear: whatever you did, you would be shot.

In the Lamine encampment there were no bugle calls to arms, no heroic fights with fixed bayonets. What the high Union command had once expected would be a major Civil War battle site had become a sleepy, out-of-the-way cantonment of troops.

# CHAPTER 6

# Private James Woodbury

From the west bluff of the Lamine River, John spotted the Lamine Bridge in the distance, with its octagonal blockhouse, inside which sentries kept watch, their rifles poking out of the blockhouse loopholes ready to repel bushwhackers.

The soldiers of Companies C and K not on guard duty were busy cleaning their rifles and preparing for morning inspection, the aroma of coffee and breakfast still in the air, when John scooted down the rocky slope of the Lamine bluffs into the cantonment. Wood smoke hung in the bottomland like fingers of fog. Several soldiers at the edge of the encampment immediately stopped him. He was out of breath, and his clothes were tattered. His arms were bloody and scratched from cutgrass and thorn bushes.

"Where is your commander?" he shouted.

They asked him to explain why he wanted to see their commander.

"I am a slave," he said.

The soldiers wanted to know from where.

"Twenty miles from here."

Why was he so out-of-breath?

He had run all the way from Sedalia, he explained. Because of the military confusion over what to do with runaways who sought refuge in Union military encampments, it wasn't entirely clear to John how he would be received by the Otterville soldiers. But whether it was true or not, he knew that if he claimed his master was a disloyal "secesh" slave owner, it would increase his chances.

Now he launched into a story that he hoped would convince the soldiers. "My owner is an officer in the rebel army."

The Minnesota soldiers did not challenge his claim, and they waited for him to go on.

"My wife and children, with other slaves, are being taken by our owner by train to Kentucky to be sold."

Who was his owner?

"Master Charles Walker."

So what was John doing at the Lamine Bridge?

"I escaped." He remembered those shots fired at him after he leaped from the platform at Smithtown and fled in the right-of-way ditch back to Sedalia.

"One of the others tried to escape with me," John said. "He was shot four times. In the head." The slave had been left dead in a ditch.

Subsequent reports from passengers on the train made no mention of a slave being shot and left dead in the railroad ditch. It may well have been a violent wrinkle John had added to the story for dramatic effect. If it was invention, he wouldn't have needed to offer it. The Minnesota soldiers had already heard stories of hungry and bloodied fugitives in tattered clothes seeking safety in Union camps from cruel masters. It took little convincing for them to imagine that John's master had shot one of his runaways repeatedly in the head.

Did he want something to eat? they asked.

There was no time! he said. The train would arrive at 9:00 a.m. in Otterville.

Several of them checked their pocket watches. What did he want them to do?

"For God's sake," John shouted again, "please save my family. This is the last chance."

They told him he would have to talk to their company commander.

"What is his name?"

Captain David Wellman, they said. They pointed to Wellman's wall tent, smoke pouring from the tent's stovepipe.

John dodged through surprised soldiers to Captain Wellman's tent. He stood at the open tent flap and repeated his appeal. He was an escaped slave. His wife and five children and other slaves amounting to thirteen all together were being "run off" to Kentucky for sale by their master. The train on which they were being transported would arrive at the Otterville station at 9:00 a.m. He wanted Wellman's soldiers to stop the train, at gunpoint if need be, remove his family and the other slaves, then send the train on its way.

John waited impatiently while Captain Wellman walked to the nearby tent of Marcus Whitman, his grizzled first sergeant, and called him out. The two men stood at the tent door and held a brief conversation.

The captain returned to his tent, and Sergeant Whitman called for his second sergeant, twenty-one-year-old Francis Merchant. Sergeant Merchant stepped inside Whitman's tent, closed the flap, then listened carefully to what Whitman explained.

"A big Negro came into camp just moments ago and asked Captain Wellman to help him secure the freedom of his wife and family and others amounting to thirteen slaves. Their master is running them from Sedalia to Kentucky on the Pacific Railroad train, scheduled to pass our camp at about nine o'clock."

Merchant checked his pocket watch. It was already getting close to nine.

Whitman went on. "The Negro also said the owner of the slaves was in the rebel army and intended to sell the slaves at auction in Louisville, before they were worthless in Missouri."

Merchant nodded to indicate he was following the story.

"Early this morning, the master tried to board the slaves in the train cars at Sedalia. But the troops wouldn't allow it. The master then went around Sedalia to Smithtown and waited to board his slaves there."

Now it was Second Sergeant Merchant who wondered what he was supposed to do.

"Captain Wellman wishes the boys to volunteer to release the slaves."

*Volunteer?* Would they be volunteering or simply following thinly veiled orders from the captain?

"The captain wants you to go speak to the boys and get them ready to go before the train arrives."

Again, Merchant checked his pocket watch.

"I want you to take command of the squad," Sergeant Whitman ordered.

Second Sergeant Merchant had the bugler sound the call for the troops to fall out. John could only stand and watch impatiently as the wheels of military decision making turned slowly.

Once the troops were at parade rest, Merchant repeated the story he had already heard from his first sergeant. Meanwhile, there had been months of confusing orders from commanders over what to do about runaway slaves. If they fled to Union camps like the one at Lamine Bridge, were the soldiers expected to simply stand aside and not interfere with the masters who came to take them back? Or could the Union armies grant the slaves safe harbor and protect them? Were soldiers required to assist neither slaves nor the slave owners searching for their property?

So what were the Minnesota soldiers supposed to do? What *could* they do, as a matter of conscience? In the morning fog and cold they were as confused as their officers over what they were expected to do about fugitive slaves and runaways. On one day, they were ordered to ignore the runaways and stand aside; the next day, they were expected to capture them and return them to their masters.

Now Sergeant Merchant explained that Captain Wellman wanted "volunteers" to go on the double-quick to Otterville and intercept the train.

Again, *volunteers*. It was a nicety that tiptoed between those who thought rescue was a duty and those who didn't want any part of it. Still, there was no doubt in the minds of some of the assembled soldiers that they were expected to volunteer. But John's dramatic story had already made its way quickly from tent to tent in the encampment. Responding to John's appeal was, some of the Minnesota soldiers felt strongly, their sacred as well as their military duty. God had ordained the rescue of slaves.

But for decades, defenders of slavery had argued that the institution was a moral blessing. Slavery was natural, they insisted, because every society had a class of people to do the menial work. They were the "mudsill" of society, the lowest of the low.

Meanwhile, the Constitution itself seemed conflicted on the issue. On one hand, it gave its blessings to justice and liberty. Yet it also declared that fugitive slaves who escaped to another state had to be "delivered up" on claim of their owners.

Ordinations by God or the Constitution, with its lofty expressions of justice and liberty, had little influence among slaveholders. "Talk, talk, talk!" John Brown had preached before he tried to invade the arsenal at Harper's Ferry to get guns to fight slavery. "That will never free the slaves," he insisted. It was time to act.

The initial action to achieve liberty and justice for slaves had been two Confiscation Acts. The first, in August of 1861, established that Union forces could confiscate the property, including slaves, of anyone who fought for or worked for the rebels. The confiscation was, the proponents of the legislation argued, a legitimate act of war and punishment for rebellious slave owners' treason. And the confiscated slaves of rebel owners were "forever free of the servitude." Those slave owners who insisted they were loyal to the Union were required to take an oath of loyalty to that effect. The Second Confiscation Act, in July of 1862, went a step further and permitted the seizure and freeing of *all* slaves whose masters, military or civilian, did not surrender to Union forces within sixty days.

Meanwhile, antislavery forces had been feuding with slavery advocates in Congress and elsewhere for a decade. One rabid proslavery senator had declared that abolitionists should be driven into desert exile like the Mormons. But radical abolitionists in Congress criticized the government for its "soft war" against slavery. They wanted an all-out assault on the institution by the government. Those who argued for the soft war were dismissed as "fossils."

President Lincoln's advocacy of a gradual and compensated emancipation that wouldn't antagonize border states and drive them into the Confederacy represented that soft war. In July of 1862 he called representatives of the border states, including Missouri, to Washington. He told them this was their last chance to accept the federal government's offer of compensation for freed slaves. If they didn't comply, Lincoln said, it would be "impossible to foresee" what disastrous events would follow. Despite the veiled threat, all of them turned the president down.

For Lincoln their refusal was the last step in his decision to go ahead with his Emancipation Proclamation, which he issued on January 1, 1863. But the proclamation freed only the slaves of those states that remained in secession. The proclamation did *not* extend to loyal border states like Missouri, which Lincoln still wanted to keep in the Union.

Union generals wondered now what to do with "this species of property" that had been seized as the contraband of war and freed or who were fugitives who had escaped from their owners. Whether runaways or contraband, what was to be done with them? In an effort to sidestep the confusion, some Union commanders banned slaves from their lines. The ban avoided having to choose between protecting them or turning them over to their owners. But one Union general argued, "Either they labor for us" or they would labor for the Confederacy. Put to work in the Union Army, they could build roads and forts and chop wood. They could be cooks and teamsters and help move supplies. It was "nigger work," and they were the ones to do it. The runaways would also make good soldiers in battle. They would fight hard to see that their families still held in bondage were set free.

Military recruiters for the Union Army spread out across the Union to find Negroes who would sign up for duty. Volunteers who were otherwise helpless swarmed into recruitment camps, signed up for service, and reveled in their newfound power as soldiers. However, some were reluctant to enlist, fearing military service as just another form of slavery. In Missouri, black men could not enlist in the Union Army until November of 1863, so they fled to other states to enlist. In those border states where slavery continued, owners locked up the shoes and clothing of their slaves at night to prevent runaways.

Some Northern newspapers praised the black troops. "They fight much better than expected," one Union general said. But Union soldiers who held Negroes in contempt said the black troops were "cowardly rascals." Still, over eight thousand slaves in Missouri signed up for military duty. Or like John, they came into Union encampments seeking help and refuge.

Thirty-six soldiers from companies C and K stepped forward and volunteered to rescue John's family. They were as young as eighteen, as old as nearly forty. They were sleepy still and bored by the tiresome military rituals of close order drill and daily inspections. For what? There were no reports of nearby bushwhackers. Rebel troops from Gettysburg to Missouri were on the run.

The volunteers were mostly farm boys from rich prairie land that invited bountiful crops and harvesting. There were no night riders or bushwhackers who came galloping past their farm outposts at midnight. There were no imperiled railroads and certainly no bridges like the one they were assigned to protect. There were no masters who hunted down runaways. There were no Negro slaves who tried to escape their bondage and then were shot like prairie jackrabbits. Some of those Minnesota soldiers had never even *seen* a black man.

Now, a breathless fugitive Negro had burst into their camp begging for the rescue of his family. Here was an opportunity to find at least temporary relief from the daily life in the Lamine encampment. It was also an opportunity for the men of Companies C and K to perform a deed that they believed was their solemn duty.

One of those who did not volunteer was Private James Woodbury, a twenty-three-year-old carpenter who had left Maine and come up the Mississippi to Minnesota via steamboat. From the Mississippi, he had walked for days through heavy rains to get to Mower County. He built a small oak-frame cabin on a quarter section of land four miles west of Austin. The soil was a rich, dark loam nearly four feet thick that he could easily sink a shovel into. He planted and cut hay, then slept on the hay with a straw tick for a blanket. He dug a cellar. He wrote his family back in Maine that he had one cow that gave him four quarts of milk a day. At night, he said, he could hear the wolves howl. From the highest prairie ridges on his land, he could see as far as fifteen miles.

When Woodbury heard the news of the Dakota outbreak in Minnesota, he was outraged and eager to help in what he considered the heroic effort to put down the uprising. The frontier should be safe for settlers, he thought, so that they could enjoy the same independence and frontier democracy he was experiencing. If soldiering meant enduring the purposelessness of close order drill and annoying sergeants barking orders at him, he was ready to do it.

But instead of fighting Indians on the Minnesota prairie, Woodbury found himself enduring the boredom of military drilling in the foggy bottoms of the Lamine River. His one relief from that boredom was using a cartridge box as a desk to write letters home to his family and his new wife, twenty-year-old Amanda Setzer, whose neighboring farm he could see from the highpoint of his own land. He had married her after a whirlwind courtship. For the ceremony, Amanda wore a gingham sunbonnet and a calico dress with wood buttons. One week later Woodbury delivered a sad goodbye to his bride and returned to his regiment.

None of Colonel Wilkin's feistiness or military discipline sat well with James Woodbury. Reveille, roll call, a quick breakfast, then two hours of morning drill, lunch, two more hours of afternoon drill, followed by a parade of marching and wheeling and turning, then supper, another roll call, finally a slow drumbeat and a bugle call to signify lights out—it was all exactly the monotony that Woodbury had feared he would have to endure in the fight to put down the Indian uprising. But the Dakota war was over. His regiment had only been part of the fight here and there. The worst Indian offenders had been hanged. Citizens who had fled their homes out along the Minnesota River were slowly returning. What was the point now of military drills day and night?

Woodbury wrote that the thought of shooting and killing rebel soldiers with whom he sympathized was repugnant. He loved the independence and democracy of farming, and he hated the idea of a military caste system. And what was the purpose of marching back and forth day after day? If it was to eliminate slavery from the Union, then Woodbury was not alone among Union soldiers who rejected that purpose. He wrote that he hoped God would end the Civil War soon. With nothing to look forward to except the unhappy prospect of going south to fight rebels, some Union soldiers were deserting. But desertion was a cowardly act he would never commit, he vowed. Still, he felt that Abraham Lincoln was determined to ruin the country. The president should be "kicked out of the Capitol," he insisted.

Woodbury was not among the volunteers who stepped forward to rescue slaves. The idea of slogging through sticky mud and then climbing up out of the Lamine bottomland to get to Otterville did not appeal to him. He had experienced a month of cold and muddy misery at the cantonment, marching and drilling and shivering. Deep snow had already fallen twice since the detachment had arrived to defend the bridge. Woodbury wrote his wife and family back in Minnesota that Missouri was colder than Mower County, to which he was eager to return.

Why was he even in Missouri in the first place, guarding a meaningless bridge that the previous defenders had surrendered without firing a shot? Meanwhile, he had not even received the twenty-five dollar bounty he had been promised at his enlistment. So why should he rush to the aid of a handful of slaves belonging to an owner who had done him no wrong?

# CHAPTER 7

# Captain Oscar B. Queen

John's sudden appearance in the Lamine encampment was the first incident of any note for the men of the detachment, and it aroused many of them out of the sleepy boredom of daily drill and guard duty. Now, with Sergeant Francis Merchant in the lead and John beside him, the detail headed for the Otterville station.

Merchant and the men, including Henry Ehmke, came up the steep slopes of the Lamine bluffs, then jogged along the Pacific Railroad tracks two-and-two with rifles at port arms, their canteens ringing like cowbells, as if they were a herd of docile Mower County Holsteins coming to the rescue instead of Union troops with fixed bayonets. They headed west for Otterville, determined to stop the train right on the tracks if it left the Otterville station before they could get there.

But the train still hadn't arrived at the station when the detail leaped up on the railroad platform. Only a handful of passengers stood waiting for the train's arrival. Those passengers immediately backed away from the rifle-bearing soldiers when they saw them. What did the presence of the soldiers mean? Were there bushwhackers on the train? Was there going to be a firefight on the platform, with minié balls flying back and forth? Would Union troops and bushwhackers be firing at each other through the train windows?

For a moment, all the confusion and conflict among

Missouri's citizens seemed to be suddenly focused on that tiny railroad platform. The state had become the site of a war within the Civil War. In the fight, "men seemed to have lost their reason." Now, the station platform at Otterville seemed ready to be the bull's-eye for one of those mindless moments.

Sergeant Merchant and his troops waited only a few minutes before a lonely whistle sounded the arrival of the train from Sedalia and Smithton. The big, black iron horse coasted into the Otterville station, its engine bell clanging loud and clear. It jerked to a stop, belching steam.

As soon as the train had stopped, the few passengers on the platform realized there would be no gunfire, and they began to board the train. Meanwhile, Sergeant Merchant split his detail in two and ordered half of the men to station themselves on the tracks immediately in front of the engine.

"Tell the engineer not to head out when the passengers are loaded," Merchant directed them. "Have him wait for orders."

Then Merchant indicated that half a dozen soldiers, among them Henry Ehmke, were to follow as he boarded any boxcars with open doors.

In the two years since emigrating from Germany, Ehmke had been on the move almost constantly. It might have exhausted him if it hadn't deepened his desire for adventure. The past month that he had done nothing but stand inspections and drill at the Lamine Bridge, protecting it from nothing but a howling, cold wind, had proved to be an irritating and restless interlude in his life as a landless nomad. Now he jumped at the chance to board the train at Merchant's side and help turn loose a huddle of slaves to a life that promised to be as free as his own.

Merchant directed John to wait on the platform with the rest of the detail. Then he and Ehmke and five others leaped up through the open door of the first of two boxcars.

They found John's family in a corner at the end of the first boxcar. Still holding his rifle at port arms, Merchant approached the corner where the slaves were sitting under the watchful eye of Charles Walker.

Walker stood up as Merchant approached. Union soldiers had already stopped him once in his efforts to board the train in Sedalia. He was certain he had evaded their blockade by boarding his slaves in Smithton. Now who were these soldiers with their weapons at the ready? And who was the tall, brazen sergeant leading them? What did he want?

Merchant spoke directly to the slaves. "You are at liberty to go your own way," he said. Then he added, as if to mollify Walker, "If you choose."

The slaves remained in the corner, reluctant to move. Uncertain whether or not his slaves would accept Merchant's invitation to leave, Charles Walker put himself between Merchant and his slaves.

A whistle blast sounded, and a thick snake of steam curled back from the engine and clouded the boxcar door.

Somewhere from the passenger cars behind them, the deep voice of a conductor called for the engineer to get moving. A hiss sounded, more steam signaling imminent movement.

The slaves stood as one. Their freedom seemed to have been secured by the forceful actions of the sergeant who was clearly in control. They began to push eagerly past Walker.

Then the deep conductor's voice rose again, this time from the boxcar door. None of them were to go anywhere, he shouted.

He jumped quickly up into the boxcar.

Confronting the slaves, he ordered them to sit back

down. Then he leaned out the boxcar door and shouted forward to the engineer that he was to get the train moving immediately, before the slaves could make their escape.

But the detail of men that Merchant had ordered to the front of the train had now formed a double picket line across the tracks, their rifles pointed at the engineer. He reached for the throttle and prepared to plow through the human barricade, the train's cowcatcher ready to shove them aside.

Several of the soldiers left the picket line, full cocked their rifles, and pointed them at the window where the engineer sat.

He stuck his hands out the engine window, signaling that he was surrendering. For the moment, the train wasn't going anywhere.

Back in the boxcar, the conductor tugged at his cap. "By what authority are you doing this?" he demanded to know.

"We have orders," Merchant answered. He made no move to produce anything to prove it.

"Do you have any officers with you?"

"We are all officers."

In Merchant's mind it was not an exaggeration. Back at the Lamine Bridge, Captain Wellman had *ordered* the men to volunteer for the duty. They were, in effect, deputies of their commanding officer. His order, backed up with the rifles of Merchant's men at the ready, was all the authority the sergeant felt he needed.

Defeated, the conductor stepped aside.

But Walker was confused and angry and still refused to move from in front of his slaves. He had a Union Army certificate permitting him to ship his slaves. Now the same army was insisting for the second time that no slave owner was shipping his slaves anywhere!

Walker flashed the certificate of shipment.

Merchant did not even bother to look at it. The certificate meant nothing to him. He was acting on orders for Captain Wellman.

Merchant turned to the slaves. On the strength of his boldness and nerve, he had prevailed in the brief encounter with the conductor. But there was no time to congratulate himself.

He motioned to the slaves to quickly exit the open boxcar door, and they began moving around Walker, who watched helplessly.

They had gone only a few steps, when another voice rose in protest from the boxcar door. "Who is the officer in charge here?"

Merchant turned to see who was challenging him now.

"I am Captain Oscar B. Queen," he said, "of the Seventh Missouri State Militia Cavalry."

Queen jumped up into the boxcar. Merchant eyed him up and down. Queen wore an imposing officer's greatcoat. But he had no shoulder straps or insignia signifying that he was an officer in the Union Army, or even the Missouri militia. If he had an officer's pistol holstered beneath his greatcoat, it would have been suicidal for him to brandish it just then.

But in the face of Queen's bold challenge, the slaves stopped moving to the boxcar door.

"I am in command of the troops in this military district," Queen said. The question was what unit were Merchant and his men from?

The Ninth Minnesota, Merchant answered. Stationed at the Lamine Bridge.

Queen explained that the companies of the Ninth Minnesota at the Lamine Bridge were part of the military subdistrict he commanded.

In that war within a war in Missouri, there were so

many shifting allegiances and fuzzy loyalties that it was difficult, if not impossible, to determine who was fighting whom. Some insisted that the entire Missouri militia was nothing but rebel sympathizers. So even if Oscar B. Queen was a captain in the Missouri militia, even if he was in command of the immediate military district, as he claimed, whose side in the Civil War was he really on?

For Sergeant Merchant, Private Henry Ehmke, and the others, sorting it all out was pointless. "We don't give a damn who you are!" they shouted.

Captain Queen glared at the men as if to say, who do you impudent soldiers think you are?

In a moment, Captain Queen was joined by another officer who leaped up into the boxcar. "I am Levi Pritchard," he said, "captain and inspector for the Central Military District of Missouri."

The title again meant nothing to Merchant, Ehmke, and the rest of the men.

Pritchard raised his voice. He wanted Sergeant Merchant to understand that he agreed with Captain Queen on the issue of forbidding the release of the slaves.

Merchant explained that he and his men were there acting on direct orders from their commander, Captain David W. Wellman.

Queen and Pritchard took a position side by side at the boxcar door, blocking the slaves. "You have no orders I know of," Queen said. "Leave the Negroes where they are."

But Merchant indicated the slaves were to begin exiting the boxcar door.

Still blocking the door, Queen sought a compromise. "Let the train go on," he said, "until we get to the Lamine Bridge." Merchant and his men could then stop the train if they wanted and escort the two Missouri officers to Captain Wellman, to whom they would vigorously protest the release of the slaves.

It seemed to be a resolution to the impasse, and there was a moment of silence before one of Merchant's detail piped up that it all sounded fine to him. But the rest of the men followed Merchant's objection to any idea of compromise, and they insisted that the slaves be released. Meanwhile, if the Missouri officers wanted to talk to Captain Wellman, or even President Abraham Lincoln, they could do as they pleased.

Again, Merchant told the slaves they were free to go. Then he used the point of his rifle to indicate that he also didn't give a damn who Queen and Pritchard were. They were to step aside from the boxcar door and let the slaves leave.

Oscar B. Queen was a native of Washington DC and the son of a veteran of the war of 1812. In the spring of 1849, at twenty-two years old, seeking the same courageous exploits of his father, Oscar and his younger brother Henry had signed on with a group called the Washington City Company, led by J. Goldsborough Bruff, an artist and adventurer who was heading an expedition from the nation's capital to the California gold country.

Before leaving Washington, Bruff and his newly formed mining company had been invited to the White House to receive good wishes for their expedition's success from President Zachary Taylor. Then Bruff and his men, including Oscar B. Queen, had paraded in Lafayette Square to the cheers of a crowd that gathered to see them off for Missouri and across the Great Plains to the gold country of California.

With high hopes for striking it rich, for six months Bruff's company marched day after monotonous day for twelve-hundred miles from Missouri to the Sierras. With their pack mules beside them, they covered seventeen miles a day, walking along the Platte River, then up the

Lassen Trail, which was "marked in human misery and death," finally to the western slopes of the Sierras.

In California they found no gold. And it wasn't long before Oscar B. Queen and the rest of the Washington City Company abandoned their leader Goldsborough Bruff in the high Sierras. Queen then joined a smaller squad of prospectors. They also found no gold. Instead, they came across dead oxen, broken wagons, and the bleached bones of prospectors who had struggled against the hardships of mining and appeared to have died clutching their gold pans.

Defeated in his mining hopes, Queen left California and returned to Missouri, where he received the news that his brother Henry, who had continued his California search for gold, had drowned in one of California's raging mountain rivers.

At twenty-four years old, Queen decided that he had experienced quite enough uncertainty and danger in his travels. He was ready to settle down to a conventional family life. In Missouri he married and soon had five children. Then, with the start of the Civil War, he had enrolled in the Missouri militia and quickly risen to the rank of captain. As an officer, he was dedicated less to the end of slavery or the preservation of the Union than he was to becoming a well-trained, obedient soldier. Now, as he stood with rifles pointed at him in the bleakness and gloom of a Pacific Railroad boxcar, he could only wonder, who were these unruly young ruffians from Minnesota who were so brazenly defying him?

# CHAPTER 8

# General Egbert Brown

Standing in the middle of the boxcar, Merchant and his men engaged in a shouting match with Queen and Pritchard and the conductor over their right to release the slaves.

"Break for the woods!" Sergeant Merchant directed the slaves.

Emily and Rachel passed the two infants they were carrying on their hips to the men beside them. Then they slid down to the train platform from the boxcar door.

After handing the infants down to the outstretched hands of Emily and Rachel, the older men helped the rest of the children out of the boxcar and then jumped to the platform themselves.

On the platform, where he was waiting as Merchant had ordered, John hugged his wife and children.

Now that the slaves were safely reunited with John on the Otterville platform, Merchant and his men broke off the argument with Queen and Pritchard and jumped out of the boxcar. The slaves immediately gathered in a tight group around Merchant, as if *he* were their new master.

They were now all fugitives. There may have been conflicting orders and considerable confusion over what the military was supposed to do about fugitive slaves, but there was no confusion over what would happen to the thirteen slaves. Rebel soldiers or a hastily formed posse of "nigger catchers" with fierce bloodhounds would try to track them down. Or they would be caught by Missouri bushwhackers, who had also captured Union soldiers and then cut off their ears and noses and blown their heads open with powder charges. If the rebels and bushwhackers could commit those kinds of atrocities against white Union soldiers, what might they do to a group of captured runaway Negroes?

Sergeant Merchant put the question to John. "Will you be all right?"

"We can take care of ourselves," John answered.

But their prospects for a successful escape did not depend only on what they could do for themselves. They could very well face circumstances they would be powerless to overcome, no matter how self-reliant they were.

Still, there was no time to give the slaves a lecture on the horrors that might await them.

"All right. Break for the woods!" Merchant repeated. "Go!"

John leading, the party of slaves sprinted for the woods. Queen and Pritchard watched from the open door of the boxcar. Merchant and his men remained on the platform, their rifles at the ready. If Queen and Pritchard or Charles Walker harbored any ideas of pursuing the slaves, they would have to overcome the soldiers and their pointed rifles to do it.

Merchant and his men watched from the Otterville platform as the slaves ran for the woods. Once in the trees they became nothing but wraithlike figures moving deeper and deeper into the woods. Then they disappeared altogether.

The conductor jumped out of the boxcar and ran to the front of the train. He shouted up to the engineer that they had a schedule to meet. They could not afford to spend another second at the Otterville station.

Certain that the slaves had made good their escape, the

half of Merchant's detail that had blocked the train's path stepped aside. The train's steam whistle sounded a long blast that gave a forlorn echo. The wheel pistons slid forward and back. The huge drive wheels spun once as if the track were greased. A series of quick, deep chuffs sounded from the bowels of the engine, as if it were gathering itself to leap forward. Then the train began to move slowly out of the station.

The conductor swung himself up on the boarding steps of the first passenger car. Merchant and his men had now gathered in a group on the platform and were slapping each other and cheering in celebration of the good deed they had done. Meanwhile, Queen and Pritchard were still standing in the open door of the boxcar, both of them looking back and glaring at the soldiers who had defied them.

One mile down the track from the Otterville station, Queen and Pritchard ordered the engineer to stop the train just before the blockhouse at the west end of the Lamine Bridge. Both men, accompanied by Charles Walker, leaped from the boxcar and slid down the bluffs into the Lamine cantonment. The three men found their way to Captain Wellman's tent and burst through the flap to confront him.

Queen gave a hurried and detailed account of what had happened at the Otterville station. For Queen it wasn't only that Walker's Negro slaves had been freed without the Missouri owner's consent. Wellman's men had also defied the direct orders of a superior officer.

When Queen finished, Wellman said, "I know nothing of this affair."

Queen was incredulous. "You didn't give the men orders?"

No, Wellman insisted, he hadn't.

Queen explained that the men had said they had direct orders from their captain.

Now Wellman grew angry. "The men acted without orders, entirely on their own responsibility!"

Queen, Pritchard, and Walker were in no position to know otherwise. On the strength of Wellman's statement, Merchant and his men had been nothing but rogue soldiers, acting on nobody's initiative but their own.

Wellman's version of events was a half-truth. He hadn't given the troops direct orders. Instead, the men had been told to "volunteer." So Wellman's insistence that he hadn't given anybody direct orders might have, for the moment, absolved him of responsibility for the incident at the Otterville station. But then he added, "The men are AWOL. They had no orders to commit any act of this kind."

Every man in the cantonment had been asked earlier that morning to fall out in formation. One by one, thirty-six of them had stepped forward to answer the call for volunteers. How could Wellman now insist they were AWOL? It was a barefaced lie, offered perhaps to bolster his claim of innocence regarding the Otterville incident. But the entire cantonment knew where the men had gone, and *nobody*, not even Wellman, had tried to stop them.

Walker insisted that he wanted his slaves back. They were his property. And Captain Wellman's soldiers were the ones who had turned them loose. Wellman must undo what his soldiers had done.

Wellman agreed to return to the waiting train at the west end of the bridge. Wellman, Queen, Pritchard, and Walker climbed back up the Lamine bluffs and reboarded the train. The slaves could not have gotten far, they felt; and they directed the engineer and the conductor to back the train to the Otterville station, where the same rogue soldiers who had foolishly released the slaves would be given the responsibility of getting them back.

The engineer and the conductor balked at the idea of backing up the train. Bushwhackers often blocked the forward passage of trains by laying railroad ties, horse-shoes, and logs on the rails. If the engineer tried to back up the stopped train, the absence of a cowcatcher on the caboose meant whatever obstacles the bushwhackers might have quickly laid behind the train couldn't be swept away. It meant the train might be trapped and the very ambush the engineer wanted to avoid would be inevitable. Finally, the engineer and the conductor argued, if they backed up the train, they would fall further behind in their schedule.

Captain Queen insisted that he wanted the train to back up, and the engineer and conductor agreed reluctantly. The locomotive had puffed steam and chuffed halfway back to Otterville when they met Merchant and his men walking down the tracks at a leisurely pace, still in a buoyant mood because of the good deed they felt they had done.

Wellman was the first to confront them. "Where are the Negroes?"

Merchant thought his captain was suggesting they had abandoned the slaves to bushwhacking predators.

Merchant wanted it clear that he and his men hadn't abandoned anybody. "We left the slaves in town," he said. "They insisted they could take care of themselves."

Walker interrupted the conversation between Merchant and Wellman. He wanted his slaves back, he repeated.

Some of the men laughed. Judging by the speed and desperation with which the slaves had disappeared into the woods, they would be halfway to Canada by then. Pursuit was too late.

The conductor insisted the train had to get moving. It still wasn't clear to Sergeant Merchant or any of his men that they had done anything wrong or disobeyed anybody's legitimate orders. And as they watched the train begin moving again and disappear down the tracks, with Queen and Pritchard and Captain Wellman aboard, Merchant and his men experienced a sense of pride for having performed an honorable and praiseworthy deed.

Early that night, Captain Oscar B. Queen returned to Tipton, Missouri, and the small encampment of officers and orderlies that served as headquarters for the military subdistrict that included Otterville and the Lamine Bridge.

Just a year earlier at the site, two slaves had sought safe harbor from their owners. When the owner and his son tried to break into the headquarters camp to take back their slaves, they were met by angry soldiers who began stoning the slave owner and his son. Now, however, only the muted voices of a spirited poker game broke the night quiet. From somewhere in the encampment a mellow violin sounded and the mournful piping of a pennywhistle rose and fell.

Queen withdrew to the privacy of his tent. He lit a single candle and then sat on a stool at a low desk in the flickering light. He picked up a quill pen with which to write the draft of a telegraph he intended to send immediately to Brigadier General Egbert B. Brown, commander of the Union Army's Central Missouri District. General Brown was strongly pro-Union and had worked to keep Missouri in the Union. He had only a horse collar of hair and gimlet eyes that reflected a thickheadedness. He was described as zealous and honest, but hardly brilliant and "not remarkably quick of apprehension." In his youth he had sailed out of the East Coast as an adventuresome whaler, but as a general he was criticized for being a hidebound traditionalist who lacked vigor in his duties to fight against rebel guerilla activities. The loss of one arm in battle made him even more cautious militarily.

Captain Queen paused a moment before he began his

telegraph to General Brown. Headquarters officers were renowned for their colossal egos and irritable dispositions. In one incident, an officer at the Second Battle of Bull Run had angrily remarked that the commanding general wasn't worth "a pinch of owl dung." So Captain Queen faced the possibility that his complaint about the incident at the Otterville station would seem petty and only irritate his superiors. But he was still too angry about the incident to worry overmuch about offending anybody.

He began writing carefully, providing the details of what had happened that morning but careful not to overdramatize the scene. A Missouri slave owner had attempted to ship thirteen of his slaves via railroad to Kentucky. The slave owner had a properly issued military permit for the shipment, but a group of Minnesota soldiers, under the direction of a "ringleader," had halted the train and released the slaves. Queen explained how he had tried to stop the Minnesota soldiers. But, he wrote, they had pointed their cocked rifles at him and defied him.

Their actions flew in the face of everything he had learned about military conduct. From the War of 1812, in which his father had fought gallantly, to that very moment in his tent in Tipton, Missouri, discipline and order were a necessity in warfare. There were chains of command to be followed. Battles were won by soldiers obeying orders, not defying them.

There had been no need, he went on, for the Minnesota soldiers to disobey army rules in order to "give expression to individual feelings." He carefully skirted the issue of what his feelings were about slavery and emancipation. Those feelings, whatever they might be, were beside the point. His legitimate orders had been defied by soldiers who said they didn't give a damn who he was. He felt it was a "high-handed outrage." He closed the telegraph by stating that he remained an "obedient servant" of his commanders. The signature was a reminder of the military obedience and discipline that he felt the soldiers had violated at the Otterville station.

The telegraph finished, Queen directed his orderly to rush it to the encampment's field telegraph tent for transmission by wire to General Brown in Jefferson City. As soon as General Brown received Queen's message, he sent a return telegraph to Queen ordering Captain Wellman to arrest the Minnesota soldiers and send them under guard to Jefferson City.

Meanwhile, the men of the rescue detail had returned to their Lamine encampment. By evening they had settled in their tents to disassemble and clean their weapons and prepare for the last inspection of the day before lights out.

Then a bugle call to fall out sounded.

A cold steam was rising from the icy pools of the Lamine River when the soldiers assembled in the center of the encampment. Now what? Was it another bugle call for them to come to the rescue of more slaves? Were they about to receive a commendation for their rescue mission in Otterville?

A small detail of cooks at a field kitchen just beyond the tents remained at their posts. Some of the men wondered if that was why they had been assembled. They were standing for another irritating roll call before they lined up at the field kitchen for a special bedtime treat of hot soup made from sheets of desiccated vegetables, which soldiers had nicknamed "desecrated vegetables." The soup was "utterly uneatable," but maybe it was the only commendation they would receive for their good deed.

Captain Wellman came out of his tent and stood before the men. However much he still wanted to return to Minnesota to attend to his parents and settle his business affairs, he now found himself at the center of a Missouri incident that had aggravated his superiors in Tipton and even as far away as Jefferson City. And perhaps beyond that.

"All parties who were engaged in the release of the slaves," Wellman said, "step forward."

Thirty-six men, including Sergeant Merchant and Private Henry Ehmke, stepped quickly forward. They had no reason to conceal what they had done. The mission had been heroic. They had released thirteen slaves and sent them on their way to a new life without slave masters to hound and bedevil them.

The thirty-six men stood at attention, braced and proud, fully expecting a commendation from their commander for what they had done.

Then Wellman spoke. "You are all under arrest for violation of the Sixth, Seventh, Eighth, and Ninth Articles of War," he said.

The men were stunned. They had only half listened when their company officers had read the articles to them every Sunday at roll call. What did those articles requiring proper soldierly conduct have to do with them? They were all good soldiers who had volunteered to save the Union.

But they knew immediately what Wellman meant. They were all being charged with mutiny.

# CHAPTER 9

# Colonel Alexander Wilkin

Early the next morning, the thirty-six men marched under guard to the Otterville station, where they boarded the same Pacific Railroad train they had stopped the day before. The train chuffed east along its regular route, passing through Tipton, where Captain Queen sat composing another telegraph to his superiors, explaining that the Minnesota soldiers were on their way to Jefferson City as ordered.

Captain Levi Pritchard, who with Captain Queen had challenged the Minnesota soldiers at the Otterville station, also sent a telegraph to Jefferson City about the incident. It was his duty and therefore his "honor," he said, to give a report on the troubling episode. The reference to "honor" wasn't just a military courtesy. He had been as offended as Captain Queen by the disobedience of the Minnesota soldiers.

Pritchard offered the same details of the incident that Captain Queen had already related. As if to absolve Charles Walker of all blame, Pritchard said the slave owner's attempt to ship his slaves to Kentucky had been done "in compliance" with the permit he had been issued by military authorities. Captain Queen had ordered the Minnesota soldiers to let the shipment proceed as ordered. But the men had refused to obey and had cocked their guns.

In Jefferson City the men arrived at the railroad station

along the Missouri River levee and were marched still under tight guard through the busy, crowded streets. Those who saw them pass in a solemn procession could only wonder if they were Union deserters. What else could they have possibly done that deserved such a strict escort? And where were they to be confined while awaiting court-martial? Makeshift jails and prisons in Missouri were already filled with secessionist firebrands. Even the wives and mothers of guerilla suspects were jailed.

The basement of an abandoned hotel in Jefferson City became the temporary jail for the Minnesota prisoners. General Egbert Brown described their confinement as "nominal, not real." But nearly half of them were young men hardly out of their teens. They were full of the abandon of youth and the wide-open freedom of prairie farms, where they had been confined by nothing but the sky and the distant horizon. As they sat now, like caged animals, in the damp, dirt-floor basement of the hotel, their confinement was anything but nominal.

What would happen to them? There were as many answers as there were men confined. They might be marched at bayonet point to a square scaffold while a fife and drum corps beat a steady rhythm. Then all thirty-six of them would be hanged at once. It would be a repeat of the ghastly hanging of the Sioux Indians that the men had watched in Mankato, except this time *they* would be the ones who thrashed in the air while they swung from the hangman's rope. Or they could be made to sit on their own graveside coffins while they were blindfolded and shot in front of their regiment. For the rest of the soldiers, it would be an object lesson against mutiny as horrifying to watch as the burning of a slave tied to a tree.

If not execution, what then? They might be suspended by their thumbs or sentenced to hard labor, digging holes and then filling them up, only to dig them again. They might be made to carry a heavy log while walking their guard post back and forth, back and forth. They might be sent to a Union prison in the Dry Tortugas, a kind of Devil's Island in the Florida Keys with only mangrove swamps and sea turtles and deadly tropical diseases. They might be made to stand on a barrel head and face the ridicule of their fellow soldiers. They might be tied and stretched onto the spare wheel of an artillery caisson. They might suffer "bucking and gagging," with bayonets tied across their mouths.

In the midst of the speculation, there were a few certainties. They had been charged with mutiny. They would be tried by a general court-martial. A panel of five to thirteen officers would judge their guilt and decide their fate for "inciting or joining" in mutiny. Whatever their eventual punishment, it would take two-thirds of the court officers to agree on it.

There was one other certainty. In the bloody standoff of ideologies between the North and the South, each side trumpeted the other's instances of desertion and mutiny while concealing their own. That Union soldiers had mutinied—no matter the cause or the good deed they thought they had done—was a Union disgrace. The less the world knew about the episode, the better.

The thirty-six Minnesota soldiers were left alone and isolated from one another, facing a conviction for mutiny. To them their confinement in the basement of an abandoned hotel was as bad as the isolation of the Dry Tortugas or even Devil's Island. What little food they received was as inedible as the food served in camp. From their basement cell they could hear the noises of commerce and life on the streets of Jefferson City, reminding them of a world of freedom and promise they had once enjoyed but might never be able to return to.

Meanwhile, the two warring factions in Missouri had

found only a small measure of peace. Elsewhere, the grand fate of the entire Union seemed to hang on the outcome of battles in such humble places as Brown's Ferry and Kelly's Ford and Raccoon Valley. Who knew or cared about a handful of mutinous Union soldiers locked up in a Missouri hotel?

The incident might have remained hidden and the plight of the Minnesota soldiers unknown if it had not been for those passengers who had been on the platform at the Otterville station and witnessed the release of the slaves. By the time these witnesses had arrived late at night in St. Louis, the episode had acquired for them the harrowing urgency of a train robbery or a derailment by bushwhackers.

The first story, which anxious passengers described to reporters in the St. Louis depot, appeared two days later in St. Louis's *Westliche Post*, which served an extensive German American community. "Another Nigger-Driver Prevented from Exporting His Chattels," the headlines read. The facts were simple: In Missouri, slave owner Charles Walker had tried to ship his slaves to Kentucky slave markets. Union soldiers from the Ninth Minnesota, many of them good German immigrants, had stopped the train and freed the slaves, who had promptly disappeared. From that first story in the *Westliche Post* reporting the Otterville incident, the news spread rapidly via telegraph in November. Newspapers in Winona, Austin, St. Paul, St. Louis, and Chicago picked up the story, and each added details.

In the meantime, President Abraham Lincoln's Gettysburg Address gave the story of the mutinous Minnesota soldiers an ironic twist. Over ten thousand people, some of them in the boxcars of freight trains, had poured into the little Pennsylvania town of Gettysburg, site four months earlier of one of the bloodiest battles of the Civil

War. The reason for the gathering was the dedication on November 19 of the battleground as a national cemetery.

On the morning of the dedication, a layer of clouds over Gettysburg suggested rain. But after the famous orator Edward Everett took over two hours to deliver his speech from a wooden platform on the highest point of the battlefield, the sun beamed brightly, and a restive crowd took advantage of the seemingly endless speech to wander around the battlefield, marked by dead horses, damaged stone walls, shell craters, and the graves of the thirteen hundred men who had been buried two feet apart in long rows that curved gracefully over the ground where some of them had fallen.

President Abraham Lincoln had been asked to speak at the dedication almost as an afterthought. Now, as he stood up and moved to the edge of the platform to speak, boards creaked in the quiet that fell. Would he also deliver a tedious, long speech? Would the huge crowd have an opportunity to drift off again and wander about the battlefield?

In a "perfect silence," Lincoln's voice rang high and clear. America had been conceived and dedicated to the proposition that "all men were created equal." The men who had died at Gettysburg had done so dedicated to a "new birth of freedom" in the nation.

The platform from which Lincoln spoke was close by the slope where brave soldiers from Minnesota's First Regiment had rushed into the Gettysburg battle with fixed bayonets to plug a gaping hole in Union lines. By the time the battle was over, the Minnesota regiment had lost 82 percent of its men, the greatest loss of any Union regiment in a single Civil War fight. They had died dedicated to a "new birth of freedom" in the nation.

In Minnesota the news of Lincoln's Gettysburg Address was all the press needed to celebrate its brave soldiers, who this time had rescued slaves in Missouri. Theirs was not a case of mutiny, Minnesota newspapers argued, but rather an attack on the very institution of slavery for which the Civil War was in part being fought. Young soldiers had enforced, at gunpoint, the Great Emancipator's noble Gettysburg proposition that all men are created equal. The men were to be commended, not jailed. In the eyes of God Almighty they had done the right thing.

The soldiers did not read the newspaper accounts of their imprisonment until two weeks into their isolation. That somebody knew and cared about them gave them hope that their imprisonment would soon end. With this renewed hope, the soldiers sought to create a firestorm of Northern protest on their behalf. By candlelight in the dankness of their basement jail several men began crafting letters to family or newspaper editors, pleading their case. They agonized over each word, scratching out and then rewriting phrases that didn't have the proper rhetorical effect. Their fellow prisoners stood by anxiously, as if watching the seesaw progress of a boxing match.

The soldiers wrote they had been imprisoned for two weeks and were subsisting on part rations. They were hungry. Some men had been made to buy food from their guards. They were highly pleased to see newspapers from their "beloved Minnesota" commend them. But the stories that were appearing in the Northern press mixed truth with falsehood. It was the men of the Ninth Minnesota who had faced danger, not the Missouri officers who had tried to stop them. Sergeant Merchant's leadership had been bold and "fearless." They were mostly farmers— German and French and Irish and English—but they were "true soldiers," all of them defending freedom and equality as bravely as other Minnesota soldiers had done at Gettysburg. What they had done on the train platform in Otterville was only their duty in the service of their country. They had obeyed both civil and military law as well as the laws of justice and humanity.

None of this mattered to Captain D. W. Wellman. He continued his argument that the men had gone AWOL and defied the orders of Missouri militia officers. Whatever happened to the men served them right. Meanwhile, two furloughs that finally had been granted to Wellman had not been enough to oversee his engineering business. He still had affairs to tend to, this time in Indiana. And his services as a bridge-building expert were considered "indispensable" to the military and were needed elsewhere. So what was he doing hidden away in the Lamine River bottom commanding rogue soldiers? The sooner he could leave that duty to somebody else, the better.

There had been no better soldier among the jailed rogues than Private Henry Ehmke. He had begun his enlistment as one more unassuming volunteer, just a tall rattlebones who had been disregarded. Only a few of his superiors had even seemed to know who he was, and those who did couldn't spell or pronounce his name. He was just one of several dozen Germans in the company, all of whom talked endlessly in their harsh tongue. Still, he had taken all his military duties seriously, even the ones that the other men found senseless. His superiors had finally taken notice, and just days before the incident at the Otterville station he had been promoted to corporal. The recognition led him to believe that he was a good soldier who could expect even more notice and promotions in the future. Now, for doing what he and others saw as their duty, the good soldier was in jail. What had he or any of them done wrong?

Sergeant Francis Merchant had as much cause as Henry Ehmke to wonder about the justice of his jailing. He had risen even faster in the ranks than Ehmke. And all of his superiors gave his name the proper French emphasis. He was Sergeant *Mer*-shaunt, reflecting the continued respect that went beyond his military merit. Even the articles in the Minnesota papers cited his bold leadership. Now Captain Wellman was insisting that the men had acted without his approval. So who *had* put the men up to the mutiny? Captain Queen's answer was that they had acted in response to their "ringleader's" directions. That was none other than Sergeant Merchant. And as the leader of the renegades, he would be dealt with even more harshly when punishment was finally meted out.

Finally, Private James N. Woodbury congratulated himself for his refusal to volunteer for the mission to Otterville. He had not stepped forward when asked because the emancipation cause seemed far removed from him. But he also had come to hate the military, and he was sick of army life, which he described as a "complete swindle." After a year of duty, from Minnesota to Missouri, he knew enough not ever to volunteer for anything. "Volunteers," Woodbury realized, wound up digging latrines or standing boring and lonely night picket duty, jumping at the sound of crickets that might have been the enemy coming to cut your throat. Volunteers could get themselves killed. Now, he and the other men were safe. Some of them even took time to hunt deer and turkeys. Meanwhile, it was thirty-six *other* men who had foolishly volunteered who would face . . . what? Long imprisonment? Worse rations than the already utterly uneatable "desecrated" ones they were getting? A court-martial in which all of them, especially Sergeant Merchant, would be broken in rank to buck privates and sent into the meat grinder of a bloody battle against half-crazed, howling rebels? Or would they all be hanged in a public spectacle?

# CHAPTER 10

# Assemblyman H. J. Fisher

Nothing the Minnesota soldiers or anyone else did had been enough to free them from jail. Newspaper editors wrote that the men had acted from the "noblest impulses of nature," while the soldiers' letters insisted that they were not to be blamed. One soldier wrote that they were all of a "quiet and orderly character."

The incident did not go unnoticed in Missouri, and the governor of Missouri ordered that no more slaves should be sent out of the state. Another legislator argued, "All the Negro wants to do is learn to read and write." If they were only given a chance to be free—the same chance the Minnesota soldiers had given thirteen slaves at the Otterville station—they would rise to the occasion. The Missouri legislature debated the idea of instructing their congressmen and senators to legislate for a Constitutional amendment banning slavery everywhere in the United States.

None of it helped. The soldiers were up against a Juggernaut, the Hindu god whose carriage had huge wheels that ruthlessly crushed even the innocent in its path. The Minnesota soldiers may not have known who or what a Juggernaut is; but as farm boys and prairie settlers, they recognized that the stark prairie seasons came and went and then came again with inescapable regularity. Facing military justice that seemed as inescapable as the seasons, the jailed soldiers felt as helpless as innocents beneath the wheels of a grinding machine. When they learned that Brigadier General Egbert Brown had ordered that the names of the guilty soldiers be verified and then sent to a specially created military commission for trial, some of them became fatalistic, believing they were doomed to suffer some kind of punishment. Whatever it turned out to be, one soldier wrote, at least they would have the "heartfelt sympathies of every Christian man and woman."

For men in their basement jail, the war news was fragmentary. The Army of the Potomac pulled back from Richmond and went into winter quarters. The Union forces at Knoxville had no winter clothing and no tents and tried to find shelter from the cold and rain and mud huddling under their ponchos. Rebels under General Longstreet threatened the Union forces at Knoxville. But inadequate provisions and the foul weather prompted Longstreet to order his army to withdraw. Elsewhere, provisions were so scarce for the Confederate soldiers that even the rats and mice had disappeared.

Back in Austin and Winona, life seemed to be carrying on as usual. There were dramatic presentations, music concerts, pantomimes. A new dry goods store on Main Street in Austin was cause for celebration: "boots and shoes," the store advertised, "sugars, flowers . . . very lowest prices." Meanwhile, as if the war were a disaster to be capitalized on, newspapers in Mower County announced cash rewards for turning in deserters.

With the arrival of the holidays, a seasonal melancholy infused the fatigue and harsh circumstances of military life. "When will this war end?" one Union soldier wrote. Another noted with envy that his family would enjoy traditional Christmas festivities surrounded by friends while he was a mere "hireling" in Lincoln's war.

Sketches that appeared in the magazines of the day aggravated the melancholy. Beside a decorated tabletop Christmas tree in her cozy living room, a Northern wife hugged her furloughed husband while his children gathered at his feet. Another Union wife looked longingly out a farmhouse window at the winter moon, while her husband on the battlefield gazed at a picture of his family.

Meanwhile, there were reports of rebel spies everywhere in Jefferson City, "chatting up treason" in the town's saloons. So why weren't they caught and jailed like the Minnesota soldiers? Meanwhile, Minnesota boys loyal to the Union remained in a hotel prison near those same saloons. And Lincoln's Proclamation of Amnesty to those who had fought for the Confederacy made matters worse. Why wasn't the same reprieve granted to the Minnesota soldiers?

The first break for the men came when a member of the Missouri General Assembly named H. J. Fisher received a letter describing the incident at the Otterville station from one of the jailed Minnesota soldiers who identified himself only as a "volunteer." Fisher was sympathetic and immediately drafted a petition on behalf of the imprisoned soldiers.

The petition was quickly signed by sixty of Fisher's fellow Missouri legislators and forwarded to General Brown. The petition requested the general's "favorable consideration" of the Otterville incident based on several grounds:

> The slave owner Charles Walker was a man who was a rebel now in arms against the Union.
>
> Neither Captain Queen nor Captain Pritchard had visible insignia identifying them as officers.
>
> The train had not been delayed beyond its usual schedule.

The soldiers had had the sanction of their superiors. The Minnesota regiment had only recently been organized, and it could hardly be expected that the men had learned the "strict military bearing and discipline" that characterized a soldier's life.

The men were all of high moral standing in the communities from which they came in Minnesota.

The men were ready to sacrifice their lives in defense of the Union.

Finally, the men were all from a free state, and it was only natural that they should hate slavery.

The legislators reminded General Brown that they were the same civil servants who had signed a petition recommending Brown's promotion to brigadier general. They wanted him to understand that as petitioners they were not reckless. He owed them a serious consideration of their appeal. They characterized their petition as a "prayer" on behalf of the soldiers. They concluded with the hope that it would meet General Brown's approval and that the soldiers would be set free.

General Brown was not moved by the petitioners' prayer, and he immediately fired back a letter to the Missouri legislators. As a citizen from a free state, he said, he abhorred slavery. But army rules could not be bent. The men were under arrest for "mutiny." The idea that the Minnesota soldiers had not been trained or disciplined was nonsense. They had been in the service of their country for over a year. Even if they were untrained, ignorance was no excuse for mutinous conduct. Without addressing the petitioners' claim that neither Queen nor Pritchard wore officer's insignia or shoulder straps that were visible, Brown insisted that both officers had been in uniform. Meanwhile, the men had violated Sections 6, 7, 8, and 9 of the Articles of War. These were offenses of "grave character," and he was not authorized to release the men.

Finding nothing sympathetic in General Brown's response, H. J. Fisher dashed off another letter on behalf of the men, this time to Missouri senator Gratz Brown, who was so ardent in his antislavery views that he had been shot in the leg in a duel over the issue. Courtesy and prayer had failed to move General Brown. Now Fisher was direct in his appeal to Senator Gratz Brown. The soldiers had been on half rations for more than a month. Their only offense was freeing the slaves of a rebel in arms against the Union. The charges of mutiny were "trumped up," Fisher wrote. The entire incident undercut the bravery and spirit of the soldiers involved.

Senator Gratz Brown's constituency in St. Louis included many German Americans who were offended by what had happened to the German American boys from Minnesota. Cognizant of his constituents' feeling and sympathetic to the soldiers' plight, Senator Gratz Brown sent a letter on behalf of the soldiers to Brigadier General Brown. Aware that public support for the soldiers was gaining momentum, General Brown gave ground grudgingly and ordered members of his staff to make an investigation of the incident. On the basis of the brief, month-long investigation, he concluded:

> The Minnesota soldiers had been "misled" by the slave John when he told them his owner Charles Walker was in the rebel army. Walker was not a rebel. He was a "loyal citizen" of the state of Missouri.
>
> Walker had a military permit to ship the slaves to Kentucky.
>
> The confinement of the soldiers was not inhumane. They were receiving full rations.
>
> Queen and Pritchard had been in uniform.

Having laid out his own version of events based on his investigation, General Brown was now prepared to be conciliatory. He left his headquarters in Jefferson City and went straight across town to the hotel basement prison.

His sudden presence in the makeshift jail surprised the Minnesota soldiers. Generals in frock coats, felt hats, and sashes were as mythical as gods, and the men stood at attention immediately.

General Brown introduced himself and began by saying that he had made his own investigation of the incident at the Otterville station. He was convinced, he said, that the men were all good soldiers who had cheerfully obeyed all orders.

He paused to let his praise have its full effect.

But, he continued, what they had done at the Otterville station was wrong.

Brown's statement was stark criticism after his high praise, and the men were confused. Where was he headed with his speech?

He got quickly to the point. Would they acknowledge the error of their actions at the Otterville station?

The silence of hesitation filled the cold basement jail.

Brown repeated that he wanted the men to acknowledge their error.

There was still silence.

If they would acknowledge their error, he said a third time, they would be released from jail.

Penitence, especially if General Brown made no effort to determine if it was real, was a small price to pay for freedom.

Yes, they said, they were sorry for what they had done.

Was the punishment they had already received sufficient to prevent further occurrences?

Now there was no hesitation. Being locked up for over

a month in a cold basement jail had been a nightmare. Yes, the punishment was sufficient, they said.

The issue of mutiny wasn't over yet. General Brown fully intended to ask his superiors in Washington to convene a military board of inquiry to investigate the matter. In the meantime, General Brown said, the men were free to return to their unit at the Lamine Bridge.

# CHAPTER 11

# Senator Morton Wilkinson

The temperature in Washington fell well below freezing to welcome the new year of 1864. For the first time in seven years the Potomac River froze. Union gunboats were set in the foot-thick ice like ships in a bottle. Enterprising vendors hurried to the Potomac to harvest the ice with ripsaws.

Despite a week and a half of bitter cold in the capital, on Monday, January 11, cabinet members, foreign ministers, representatives, and senators prepared for a week of "elegant parties" to celebrate the new year. The late-night celebrations meant that some senators hoped they could dispense with Monday's business quickly and adjourn early in order to prepare for the celebrations of the evening.

The proceedings that day in the Senate opened at noon with nearly all fifty-two senators present. They sat in successive curved rows, each of which was gently elevated to provide a clear view of Vice President Hannibal Hamlin, presiding as president of the Senate. Hamlin overlooked the senators from a recess in one wall of the Senate Chamber with a fixity that made him look like niche statuary. Prior to his election as vice president, Hamlin had represented Massachusetts in the Senate. He knew the intricacies of Senate parliamentary procedure well. He was a powerful orator with a husky frame, and his strong voice directed the senators to stand for a prayer by the senate chaplain.

It was not unusual at legislative and civic ceremonies for clergymen to offer long, earnest prayers that exhausted the spirituality of the listeners. But on this day, the chaplain's prayer was brief, in recognition of the senators' wishes for a short session. Following the prayer, one by one, senators rose to offer nine separate and seemingly insignificant petitions, ranging from a request from New York Quakers to be exempted from the military, to Pennsylvania farmers who wanted compensation for property destroyed in battle.

Following the petitions, a bill was introduced asking that a portion of Texas be set aside for persons of African descent. The bill was in response to those who had been arguing that the only solution to the problem of racial strife in the United States was the removal of Negroes to colonies. This was an explosive issue that suggested extensive debate. But the bill was promptly referred to committee.

The importance of the proceedings gained more significance when Missouri senator John Henderson stood to introduce a joint resolution by the Senate and House for a Constitutional amendment to abolish slavery in all of the United States, not just those rebel states singled out in Lincoln's Emancipation Proclamation. "Nothing short of a Constitutional amendment," Henderson said, "will give freedom to black millions."

A Constitutional amendment? This was serious business and invited hours of soaring oratory from senators. But again, what should have led to a lengthy and boisterous debate was referred to committee.

Hannibal Hamlin let his gaze wander among the senators. They had been in session less than an hour. The prospects of a long, tiresome session when the rest of Washington was preparing for an evening of gala parties seemed avoided. Some of the senators fidgeted, anxious to adjourn for the day.

Then forty-five-year-old Senator Morton Wilkinson from Minnesota suddenly rose and requested to be recognized. The balding Wilkinson had thin, squeezed lips that reflected repressed emotions. Those emotions periodically boiled to the surface on the Senate floor, and another senator had once scolded Wilkinson during debate for "not knowing what he says when he gets excited." He was a passionate opponent of slavery and had vowed to "do everything in my power towards its final extinction."

Now he took a deep breath to make sure his emotions were in check. "Mr. President," he said levelly, "I offer the following resolution, and ask for its present consideration."

Present consideration of a resolution? This could mean endless debate and oratory. More murmuring rose from the Senate floor.

Hamlin banged his gavel again. When he had silence, Wilkinson began to read.

"The Secretary of War," he said, "is hereby instructed to inform the Senate whether he has any official information in his department relating to the arrest and imprisonment in Missouri of a large number of soldiers of the Ninth Minnesota Regiment."

What had been murmuring was now a rumble of voices.

A few senators were already familiar with the issue Wilkinson was raising. But for the rest, Wilkinson's resolution was too general and vague to do anything but be intriguing. Union soldiers? Arrested? Jailed? For what? By whom? Despite the rush to adjourn, this could be important business. The senators wanted to hear more, and Hamlin immediately received unanimous consent for consideration of Wilkinson's resolution.

All eyes turned to Wilkinson now for the details.

The Ninth Regiment of Minnesota soldiers, he began, had been recently sent to guard a railroad bridge in Missouri. "A few days after they were encamped," he continued, "a Negro runaway slave named John had come into the camp and told the soldiers that he was a free man, and that his master had gone into the service of the Confederate government."

Wilkinson paused to let his audience appreciate the good-versus-evil elements of his story.

Then Wilkinson went on. The Negro slave told the soldiers that his Confederate master was sending his slaves via train to the South for sale, but he had escaped and come to the soldiers for help. The soldiers from the "pure atmosphere of Minnesota" thought that this was an outrage, and about forty of them started for the depot, found the train, and delivered the slaves to the Negro John, who was "their husband and father."

Good husbands and fathers versus rebel slavers! The story drew even sharper lines of good versus evil.

"Forty of these soldiers," Wilkinson said, "were arrested and put in prison."

Wilkinson had delivered the narrative in a calm voice. Still, his sense of drama was rising, and in a forceful voice he read a letter he had received from one of the imprisoned soldiers, who wrote that "proslavery tyrants" in Missouri were responsible for their incarceration.

Then Wilkinson explained that he had received a second letter from one of the members of the Ninth Regiment who had not been imprisoned. The writer complained that Minnesota soldiers in Missouri had been put in ball and chain and "compelled to drag them around the camp." Wilkinson paused to gather his emotions. "These things in the state of Missouri must stop!" he shouted. Minnesota soldiers should not be imprisoned to "gratify the pro-slavery feelings of the officers in command of that state." Were these outrages being done on the initiative of local military authorities, he asked, or "under the sanction of the authorities here in Washington?"

The allegation was serious. Had Abraham Lincoln's own government approved the actions in Missouri?

Wilkinson had not yet received the news that the Minnesota soldiers had been released from their basement prison a month earlier, and he continued with his voice rising. The Minnesota regiment, he said, "will be utterly demoralized if these soldiers are not released from their confinement." They were "as good a regiment as could be found anywhere in the Army."

Having drawn sharp lines between good and evil in Missouri and having enlisted the sympathies of most of the senators, Wilkinson conceded that perhaps the Minnesota soldiers had committed "some little act of insubordination to General Egbert Brown, who was in the railroad car."

Only Captains Queen and Pritchard had been in the railroad car, but Wilkinson's version of events went unchallenged.

"If we want these men to fight," Wilkinson went on, "they must be treated a little differently." The point of his resolution was to discover what had really happened at the Otterville station and the Lamine Bridge. His voice rising, Wilkinson concluded, "I will never consent that [Minnesota soldiers] be made the tools of slavery-loving tyrants of Missouri."

Wilkinson sat down. His description of what had happened in Missouri to heroic Minnesota soldiers stood as a shocking case of abolitionist justice versus slavery evil.

Kansas senator James Henry Lane was the first to rise in response to Wilkinson. He had wild, unkempt hair and had earned the nickname the Grim Chieftain, because of his fierce, brutal leadership of military campaigns against proslavery towns in Kansas. He was said to have "no equal as a stump orator"; and when he wasn't railing against the proslavery forces in Kansas, he was leading a unit of "Jayhawkers" into Missouri to fight Confederates. His daring exploits made him heroic among abolitionists, whose rallying cry was "Hurrah for Jim Lane."

The report that Union soldiers were being jailed was nothing new to Senator Jim Lane. He had something to say on that subject. "Scores if not hundreds of soldiers have been confined in the guard houses of Missouri," Lane said, for no other offense than hurrahing for Jim Lane. In fact, Lane said, two soldiers in Missouri had been bayoneted for the offense.

Soldiers bayoneted in Missouri for their abolitionist outcries? If it was true, it was another outrage, and Massachusetts senator Charles Sumner jumped to his feet.

Sumner could be as fiery in his abolitionist convictions as Jim Lane. In a quarrel on the Senate floor about slavery, an angry colleague had beaten Sumner nearly to death with a cane. The senator had spent three years recuperating before he could return to the Senate. He could be irascible and intransigent, and he was not about to ignore the news that loyal Union soldiers were being bayoneted in Missouri.

"By whose order?" he demanded to know.

Still standing, Senator Lane ignored the question of who might have ordered it. Five soldiers had been arrested in Missouri on the offense of having shouted "Hurrah for Jim Lane," he insisted. Two of them had been bayoneted while they were being forced into jail. The senators erupted with anger.

Once more Vice President Hamlin had to gavel the senators to order.

Lane turned now and spoke directly to Senator Wilkinson. He expressed his gratitude to Wilkinson for drafting and introducing the resolution that would call the incident at the Otterville station to the attention of the War Department and the president. Then Lane sat down.

Finally, Missouri senator John B. Henderson rose. With a huge bow tie and a watch chain that dangled conspicuously beneath his vest, he cut a dashing figure.

"I desire the resolution be passed," Henderson said. There were no objections, and the resolution passed quickly. It was now up to President Lincoln and his secretary of war, Edwin M. Stanton, to investigate the incident at the Otterville station and decide what to do with the Minnesota soldiers who were involved.

# CHAPTER 12

# General John McAlister Schofield

For three years President Abraham Lincoln had been troubled by the fight over slavery in Missouri. The fight had been a war within the war, and the president had anguished over what he could do that would satisfy the antislavery radicals yet not alienate Southern sympathizers. He felt that those antislavery radical forces in Missouri were unhandy "devils" to deal with but that they were "nearer to me than the other side," who continued to defend slavery and resist Union control.

Yet he saw both factions as dangerous and pestilential. He said it was painful to him that the factions in Missouri would not or could not stop quarreling. "I have been tormented beyond endurance for months," he said. And neither of the two factions would listen to his appeals for reason and reconciliation.

"I am compelled to take hold of the state," Lincoln finally said. But what was he to do? Crack down on the proslavery forces and drive all the border states into the Confederacy? Or let border states like Missouri adopt their own plan for the gradual elimination of slavery?

Whatever he tried was treated as either tyranny or weak appeasement. He was either too hard or too soft.

Then there had been guerillas and bushwhackers, who would not stop terrorizing the citizens. Their actions had divided the state even more. To some, they were considered heroic freedom fighters; to others, pathological killers who made the rivers of Missouri run red with blood. They were beyond the reach not just of Lincoln's appeals for reason. In their wooded hideouts and sanctuaries, they were even beyond the reach of the Union forces who tried to hunt them down.

Beyond the trouble with irreconcilable factions and fearsome bushwhackers, there was the ineptness and fractiousness of the Union Army leadership in Missouri. Lincoln had appointed one general after another with the task of calming the divisions in Missouri. But after years of factionalism and quarreling over slavery in that state, military leadership for the Department of Missouri had proved "too difficult a task" for a succession of generals, each of whom had thrown his hands in the air, one complaining to Lincoln, "It is not for me to settle such serious controversies."

Despite the seeming inability of anyone to settle the turmoil in Missouri, the president kept looking for that one man. He finally turned to Major General John McAlister Schofield in the hope that he would be the one to resolve Missouri's problems. Schofield had a baby face, soft eyes, and long sideburns that flowed neatly into a mustache that seemed to gently cradle his chin. Schofield had been born in New York and was a West Point graduate, but he was also a professor of philosophy and physics. He believed that stern or harsh treatment of the troops in his command only inspired hatred. He had won a Medal of Honor for "conspicuous gallantry leading a regiment" in a charge against rebels during a critical battle.

General Schofield had held various commands in Missouri from the start of the Civil War. He seemed to have the right combination of firmness and understanding to straighten out Missouri. But he had immediately faced intense criticism from the press and the public. The time had passed, he said, for guerillas to be treated as if they were engaging in honorable warfare. They were to be captured and shot on the spot. Then he ordered all rebels and rebel sympathizers in the state to pay for the damages done to property and persons by the guerillas. The heirs of those Union soldiers killed by guerillas in Missouri battles were to receive five thousand dollars for each person killed. Finally, he called for the enlistment of all ablebodied men in Missouri between eighteen and forty-five to help put down the guerillas.

Some of the criticism that Schofield faced had been focused on the incident at the Otterville station. "Does not General Schofield understand?" the critics said. "We are not fighting to maintain slavery." Mower County newspaper editors had written that Minnesota soldiers did not feel disposed to fight for slavery "or slavery's fools."

Blaming Schofield entirely for the incident at the Otterville station was unfair. He hadn't been the one who had ordered the Minnesota soldiers arrested. Their arrest had been carried out by Captain Wellman on orders from General Egbert Brown. Schofield's responsibility for those orders was so distant as to be nominal. Yet he was the commander of the Department of Missouri. Didn't he understand that the Minnesota soldiers were simply putting a stop to an unlawful act approved by the officers in his command?

With criticism of General Schofield's leadership mounting, in January of 1864 President Lincoln relieved the general of his command. The temperature at General Schofield's headquarters in St. Louis dropped to below zero. A foot of snow fell. "Sleighing is splendid," the newspapers reported. In the cold and snow, General Schofield bid farewell to his troops. The serious controversies in Missouri had not been settled by General Schofield. Among his last actions as commander was to forward all documents on the Otterville incident to President Lincoln and his secretary of war, Edwin Stanton, who, in response to the Senate's resolution, had just begun to compile a report on the incident.

Through all the difficulties in Missouri, the fate of the Union had hung in the balance. Now the same military whose timid prosecution of the war and failures in Missouri had disappointed the president again, and again that military was ready to prosecute a group of Minnesota soldiers for mutiny. When would the difficulties in Missouri end?

# CHAPTER 13

# Secretary of War Edwin M. Stanton

Secretary of War Edwin Stanton had once called Lincoln "that damned long-armed ape," and the two of them side-by-side—Lincoln bony and tall, Stanton heavy and squat—were described as "two figures from comic opera." The press accused Stanton of "reckless mismanagement" of the war. They said he had caused men to be "heedlessly murdered." Despite the criticism, Lincoln called Stanton "the rock on the beach of our national ocean." And he turned now to that rock to decide the fate of the Minnesota soldiers.

While Stanton's War Department spent January and February of 1864 gathering documents for Stanton to prepare his report to the U.S. Senate, the men of Companies C and K of the Ninth Minnesota left their camp in the bitter cold at the Lamine Bridge. As soon as the bridge was abandoned, guerillas burned it a second time. Years after the war ended, the outlaw gang of Jesse James burned the bridge a final time, an ignominious end to what was once expected to be a heroic battle site of the Civil War.

The men of Companies C and K, including the men involved in the Otterville incident, headed west for Warrensburg, Missouri, with two other companies detached from the Ninth Regiment. For the first ninety miles, the four companies rode in cold boxcars, bunched for warmth in the corners like the desperate slaves rescued in Otterville. They marched the final thirty miles, fording icy creeks and streams along the way. The detachment finally made camp alongside the Blackwater River three miles north of Warrensburg, where, under Captain Wellman's leadership, they took up the work of rebuilding and guarding another bridge that had been burned.

In Warrensburg, citizens complained that some of the men were discharging their firearms in town, "to the great annoyance of the citizens." Then in a dispute over the sale of liquor, an Irishman was shot in the head by a soldier and killed. The two incidents suggested that the Ninth Minnesota was an unruly mob. Meanwhile, military authorities promptly caught and jailed the soldier. To the men at Warrensburg, there was "no doubt that he would be shot." To the men involved in the Otterville incident, that same fate seemed to be still hanging over their heads.

The bridge repair was again dull work, relieved only by annoying dress parades that seemed to have little or nothing to do with bridge building or war. Then in mid-February the weather turned warm and pleasant, almost "like spring again," inviting the men from Mower County and Winona to daydream about the arrival before too long of spring back home.

Sergeant Francis Merchant, who had led the soldiers at the Otterville station, began thinking about spring chores. He had saved a little of his military pay, but he knew that the rich soil of his quarter section had already helped him prosper. If he could escape the cloud of imprisonment hanging over his head, he would return to the log home on his family's quarter section and relieve his aging father of the responsibility of working the land. Parts of his land were still untouched by the plow. When he got back home, he would break the sod and plant more wheat. He would plant corn and potatoes. He would nurture the windbreak grove of sapling oak and maple and cottonwood that he had planted to protect the crude log home. He would build a barn. And one day he would build a roomy wood frame farmhouse with lightning rods like church spires that would take the flashes of prairie lightning and stab them into the ground like pitchforks, while inside the house they stayed safe and warm.

The fear of returning to prison also hung over Corporal Henry Ehmke's head and interrupted his thoughts of one day returning to Winona. In Minnesota the regiment had hardly stayed put for more than a month or two before they moved on again. Now they had spent eight months being shuttled from one end of Missouri to the other, doing the safe but boring work of guarding bridges. There were rumors that they were heading farther south again, for Tennessee or into the Deep South of Alabama or Mississippi, places as strange and foreign as any Henry Ehmke could imagine. But Ehmke had had enough. For the first time in his life he wanted to be settled, rooted, and at rest. Winona was as good a place as any for that. It was a river town, with travelers who came and went, headed for the promise of Edens farther west. But for Ehmke, Winona was Eden. There were lumber mills and shipping companies and flour mills. Once the war was over, he would find a permanent place in Winona's commerce. Meanwhile, young women also came and went and then came back again, because the frontier hadn't been Eden after all. For Corporal Ehmke, the ungainly, lop-eared bachelor, Winona offered the prospect of courtship and marriage. Winona, with all its noise and bustle, offered him peace.

The rumors of going south to the battlefields of Tennessee or Mississippi irritated Private James Woodbury. All he wanted was to return home to Mower County to be with his wife, Amanda. During the two-week furlough that the entire regiment had received before heading south that previous fall, he had gone to his Mower County farm to be with her. The furlough had been a short rendezvous during which he had resumed intimacies that he had enjoyed all too briefly after his marriage. But it had been long enough for the two of them to listen to the meadowlarks and the sweet whistle of prairie bobwhites. Riding into Austin for supplies, they marveled at the last of the bright goldenrod blooming along the wagon trails. At night they could see the glow of lighted candles from nearby farms. Every moment had been an enticing prelude of things he would be able to enjoy at his leisure when he finally got back home.

But now Woodbury sat at night in his cold tent beside the Blackwater Creek, his fingers too stiff to write often to Amanda. Working on the bridge in a heavy rain, he caught a cold and again reported to sick call. In the letters he found the warmth to write, he complained that it had been five months since his regiment had been paid. "If Uncle Sam can't pay up any better than that," he wrote, "he better send us home."

Still waiting to hear what was in Secretary Stanton's report on Otterville, the detachment of the Ninth finished rebuilding the bridge over the Blackwater Creek in a matter of weeks. The project gave Captain Wellman, whom the army now considered a bridge building expert, an opportunity to hector his superiors again about receiving a furlough to return home to take care of his business and his family.

Meanwhile, like a bantam rooster itching for a good fight to prove his bravery, Colonel Wilkin, the regiment's commander, proudly wrote his father in late January that he had had an audience with General Ulysses S. Grant, who came to Jefferson City to see his ailing son. A West Point graduate, Grant had risen through the ranks from the start of the war. He had earned a reputation as an aggressive commander, but his character was tarnished by persistent rumors of drunkenness. In the face of the rumors, Lincoln said if he knew Grant's brand of whiskey, he'd send it to his other generals. After leading successful campaigns at Vicksburg and then Chattanooga, in October of 1863 Grant had assumed command of the entire western war front.

In Jefferson City, Grant was "feted and petted."

Apparently, Wilkin had met Grant previously, and he wondered now if Grant remembered him.

Yes, Grant said, he did, without adding that it was Wilkin's tiny frame that was most memorable.

Wilkin got right to the point. He remained proud of his regiment. They were "looked upon as something wonderful." No other regiment could compare to it, not even the Minnesota First, which had held the line during the Gettysburg battle. Now he wanted to get his regiment, which had already been praised to Grant, out of the inaction of Missouri and into a good fight.

"I would very much like to have you with me," Grant told him.

Grant promised to do what he could to get the Ninth Regiment into action. Meanwhile, Wilkin also presented his case to the War Department and Stanton for leading his regiment into battle. Wilkin's appeal prompted some of the men of the Ninth to hope that if they did see action, Wilkin would be "the first man shot."

While the War Department listened to Colonel Wilkin's appeals on behalf of his regiment, Secretary Stanton continued to put together the report the Senate had ordered on the Otterville incident. Privates, generals, legislators, newspaper editors, and citizens from Washington to Illinois to Missouri to Minnesota had submitted statements for the report. Their versions of what had happened at the Otterville station were as far apart as they were.

Captains Queen and Pritchard and General Egbert Brown insisted that the Minnesota soldiers had mutinied. Yes, Stanton's report established, the men had believed it was their duty to rescue the slaves in the service of God and their country. But in so doing they had defied the legitimate orders of two Union officers from Missouri.

Not long after submitting a statement for the report, Captain Oscar B. Queen found himself fighting for his life. A Confederate force of two thousand men had advanced from the east on the little town of Sedalia. Queen and his small company of thirty-three mounted cavalry were ordered to gallop to Sedalia and join a citizens militia in defense of the imperiled town.

The officers commanding the defense of Sedalia put Captain Queen and his men on the east end of town, just beyond the Sedalia train depot where Charles Walker had been denied the opportunity to ship his slaves to Kentucky. Queen and his company were ordered to throw up breastworks, dig entrenchments, and hold back the advancing rebel column. Behind him, along Sedalia's streets, the bulk of the defenders also dug in. It seemed an impregnable defense. But no sooner had Queen and his men dug in than did the attacking rebels begin lobbing artillery shells over them into the center of town. Militiamen and citizens abandoned the town and fled. Their departure left Queen's little company of determined men alone to defend Sedalia.

Capitulation was quick. Rebel forces occupied the town, surrounded Queen and his men, and took them as prisoners. The rebels marched them to the platform of the Sedalia station. There, one of the rebel commanders immediately offered to release them, in return for which Union commanders would release rebel prisoners. All Queen and his men had to do was to swear an oath that they would "not again take up arms" until the prisoner exchange was completed. If they did and were captured again, they would be killed.

After taking the oath, Queen and his men were then released and made their way back to Jefferson City. There, Queen submitted a report on his surrender in Sedalia. In it he complained that he and his stout force had been deserted. It was a repeat of the predicament he had faced at the Otterville station, where he had found himself holding fast to military principles. At Sedalia he had held to those same principles, while the militiamen behind him committed another outrage, this time of retreat. Despite his bitterness, he remained faithful to his creed of military discipline, and he wrote that he was respectfully awaiting orders to return to combat.

A heavy rainstorm turned the capital streets gummy, and the Senate chambers smelled of the mud dragged in on the shoes of the senators. It was Friday, March 4, 1864, and there was fresh war news. In Mississippi a small band of rebel guerillas dressed in Federal uniforms had surprised an entire company of Negro infantry and killed them all. Some of the Negro troops were shot through the head while on their knees begging for mercy. And there were reports from Union prisoners in Virginia that they were being treated like "cattle in a slaughter pen."

The news was disturbing; and Vice President Hamlin, presiding over the Senate, had to bang his gavel hard and ask for silence in order to receive the chaplain's prayer for the day. To open the Senate's deliberations, Hamlin held up an eight-page letter from Secretary of War Stanton. The letter was, Hamlin explained, Stanton's expected report on the arrest and imprisonment of soldiers belonging to the Ninth Minnesota Regiment.

After months of uncertainty, after months of charges and countercharges, after months of the Minnesota soldiers waiting to see if they would be executed for mutiny, their fate depended on one man, Secretary of War Edwin Stanton, and the contents of his report. Few of the senators in the chamber that day could have guessed what was in this report.

The incident at the Otterville station had the potential of engaging any of the medley of traits in Stanton's character. As a young Quaker, Stanton had been made to swear "eternal hostility to slavery." Yet his commitment as Secretary of War to protect military discipline could overshadow his compassion. He had once listened patiently to the pleas of a mother and her children to spare the life of a condemned Union deserter. When the woman was done pleading, Stanton had said dryly, "The man must die." Would his report to the Senate insist that the Minnesota soldiers had violated military discipline and must now face execution for mutiny? Or would it conclude that the soldiers had honorably and compassionately come to the rescue of slaves?

The incident at the Otterville station inflamed the emotional hearts of both those who opposed and those who defended slavery. The fiery controversy invited Stanton not to report anything that would further inflame either side. So would the report wind up as just another innocuous political document that had been appropriately ordered to "lie on the table" and gather dust?

Finally, reports and congressional investigations typically took months if not years to complete. But here was Stanton's report after just seven weeks. Few who knew his prodigious capacity for work would have been surprised. He was "the man in a hurry." His ability to immerse himself in work fifteen hours a day while standing, rather than sitting at a desk, might have been seen as an effort to suppress the grief in his life. In a short five-year period before the war, he had lost his only daughter, his only brother, and also his wife, Mary. After the death of his wife, his grief "verged on insanity," and he wandered his house calling for Mary. Would Stanton's report reflect that he had finally caved in to all the grief of his life, leading to a report full of incoherent confusion?

Stanton's report made one thing clear. The responsibility for the charges against the Minnesota soldiers lay with Captains Queen and Pritchard, Captain Wellman, and General Egbert Brown. Each had had a hand in initiating the imprisonment; and each continued to insist, despite the Northern press's editorials in support of the Minnesota troops, that the full measure of military law needed to be enforced, because the soldiers had disobeyed superiors. On General Brown's orders, formal military charges against the soldiers had been drawn up. Meanwhile, Queen's and Pritchard's written statements of outrage over the incident had been forwarded to Secretary Stanton, to be included in his report.

From the very start, Captain Wellman had refused to support his own troops, and he did not submit a statement to Stanton for the report. Wellman's efforts to distance himself from the incident left the Minnesota men without a single military advocate. Meanwhile, their most vigorous defenders were the Northern newspaper editors and the Missouri legislators, who had been the first to take up their cause.

Stanton's report contained a letter from a private in C Company who explained that the officers had had no mark of rank visible and that the men hadn't recognized them as officers. But General Egbert Brown insisted in the report that both officers, Queen and Pritchard, had been in uniform.

If that was true, the report pointed out, then their overcoats had hidden their shoulder straps.

Even if Queen's and Pritchard's rank had been visible,

Pritchard's letter on the incident explained that the men hadn't given a damn who Queen and Pritchard were. They were accused of being proslavery. They were not truly loyal officers who were living up to their obligations to defend the Union. And the owner of the slaves was guilty of treason, because he was serving in the Confederate Army.

General Brown disagreed again. In the report, he insisted that Charles Walker was a loyal citizen of Missouri. Meanwhile, the only thing Queen and Pritchard had an obligation to do was to see that Walker had a permit from the military authorities in Sedalia to ship his slaves. It didn't matter that an order prohibiting him or anyone else from shipping Negro slaves out of the state of Missouri had been issued. The military authorities at Sedalia had never received that order. And in the absence of any orders, Charles Walker had a right to do what he pleased with his slaves.

The report included other letters written by the soldiers while they were confined in the basement of the hotel in Jefferson City. Their letters maintained that they had acted upon orders from their superiors. They thought they were obeying the law. They insisted in the report that a direct order had been issued by Captain Wellman to Sergeant Merchant to release the slaves.

To counter claims that Sergeant Merchant was no better than a damnable ringleader, Assemblyman H. G. Fisher wrote that Merchant was a brave soldier. He had led an attack on slavery. Merchant had been ordered, Fisher said, to see how many men would volunteer for the rescue detail. Those who volunteered were men of high moral standing in their communities. They were all honest men. They were all quiet soldiers. They were all good citizens. They were from the free state of Minnesota. It was natural that they should abhor slavery. There wasn't a soldier or Christian in the North who didn't have sympathy for them.

In the report, General Egbert Brown was adamant in his disagreement: a soldier's personal feelings were no reason for him to set aside his duties or defy army regulations. What they had done was a high-handed outrage. They had cocked their guns and threatened to shoot the engineer of the train. It was mutiny.

The Missouri legislators who had been the first to defend the Minnesota soldiers argued just as adamantly in the report that mutiny was a "trumped up charge." The men had acted under the noblest impulses of nature. They had been ready to sacrifice their lives in defense of their country. Whatever punishment was meted out to them would be a crown of glory on their heads.

Had or hadn't a slave been shot? Had or hadn't the men been issued an order by their superiors to rescue the slaves? Had or hadn't Captains Queen and Pritchard been recognized as Union officers? Had or hadn't the Union troops in Sedalia received the order prohibiting the shipment of slaves from Missouri? Was or wasn't Charles Walker loyal to the Union?

General Brown conceded in the report that the facts in the case were confusing, and he asked in the report to Stanton that a board of inquiry be convened to separate truth from falsehood. But it did not take long for Secretary of War Edward Stanton, the "man in a hurry," to understand that a plodding board of inquiry was no solution. Stanton was the "rock on the beach" of the Union, and now he gave his judgment on the incident at the Otterville station with characteristic bluntness.

"The application by General Brown for a board of inquiry is disapproved," he ended the report. "The interests of the service do not require further action be taken in the matter."

CHAPTER 14

# Taps

After the thirty-six soldiers of the Ninth Minnesota received the news of Stanton's dismissal of the charges of mutiny against them, there was hardly an opportunity for them to celebrate the news. As soon as they finished rebuilding the bridge over the Blackwater River, they made their way to St. Louis, where the scattered elements of the Ninth came together for the first time. In St. Louis, after weeks and months of promoting his regiment's discipline and battle readiness, a determined Colonel Wilkin had managed to get the Ninth included as part of an eight thousand–man force that would head for battle in Mississippi.

At last the Ninth would see combat, the realization of Colonel Wilkin's dreams. Prior to their departure Wilkin made the men march in one more irritating dress parade, to demonstrate their combat readiness. The occasion was the "Ladies' Great Sanitary Fair" in St. Louis, sponsored by an organization of women dedicated to raising money to aid Union soldiers gravely wounded in battle. Parading before this huge crowd stood as a weak display of the Ninth Regiment's courage. Meanwhile, the regiment's one heroic moment, at the Otterville station, went unrecognized.

On May 29 the expedition left St. Louis by train, disembarking at Memphis. Then for nine straight days, the expedition, including the soldiers of the Ninth Minnesota, marched south through rain and along muddy roads. Captain D. W. Wellman was not with them. On the basis of his successful bridge building, the captain had been relieved of his duty with the Ninth and appointed as a topographic engineer in Missouri. This promotion meant that while the men of companies C and K marched day after day to reach the battlefield, the captain who had done his best to distance himself from the incident at the Otterville station was even further removed from the soldiers he had led. He had done nothing to defend the imprisoned soldiers, and he continued to insist that he had had no part in what had happened.

Still, back in Missouri, one-armed General Egbert Brown wrote that Wellman was a "good officer" who deserved promotion. Then Brown, whose petition for a military board of inquiry into the incident at the Otterville station had been denied, was relieved of his command of the Central District of Missouri for failing to obey a superior's order to attack rebel forces in Missouri. With Brown's removal, the two men who had been most instrumental in advocating punishment for the Minnesota soldiers were permanently removed from the incident.

After marching south from Memphis, the expedition reached a point a few miles north of Brice's Crossroads in northern Mississippi. Friday, June 10, 1864, dawned hot and sultry, and the men awoke still exhausted and sore from their long march. For the men of the Ninth, dreams of a bright, clear spring in Minnesota were gone. This was the steamy and heavy tropics. This was like the sweaty desolation of the Dry Tortugas in the Florida Keys, where the men behind the Otterville incident might have been imprisoned had it not been for the judgment of Secretary Stanton.

As soon as the men of the expedition were in formation that morning, they were ordered to march to an open field of battle at Brice's Crossroads. During the march, they could hear the boom of battlefield artillery, an indication that the rebel infantry and cavalry were on the battlefield in force.

In fact, the battle forces at Brice's Crossroads were lopsided. Union infantry and cavalry numbered over eight thousand men. Rebel cavalry and infantry, under the brilliant tactical leadership of General Nathan Bedford Forrest, numbered just five thousand men, but those forces had the upper hand in the pitched battle.

Union cavalry, in the thick of the battle, had fought for three hours and were exhausted. The infantry men of the expedition were directed to continue their march on the double-quick to an open field at Brice's Crossroads and relieve the cavalry.

At 2:00 p.m. the infantry forces of the expedition, including companies C and K of the Ninth, rushed forward onto the open field. In the hot sun, many men fell out of ranks and fainted. Union cavalry formed a line in front of the infantry and repelled a rebel attack. But a second attack by the rebels put the spent Union cavalry in retreat. At 2:00 p.m., after their double-quick march, the sweaty and exhausted infantry of the expedition took over the line and threw the rebels back for a second time.

Nathan Bedford Forrest spotted the exposed flanks of the Union infantry and executed a classic double envelopment that closed around the Union troops like a steel animal trap. The only path of retreat north for the Union forces at Brice's Crossroads was a narrow causeway over swampy ground. The rush by thousands of troops to get through the bottleneck of escape began at five o'clock in the afternoon and was marked by confusion and panic. As the men retreated, it was Colonel Wilkin and his brigade, among them the Minnesota soldiers, who defended the rear and kept the rebels at bay while the rest of the expedition fled.

In their eagerness to get away, many of the men of the expedition shed rifles, ammunition, haversacks, and food. Ambulances with the wounded became mired in the mud and were abandoned with men begging "piteously" for water. That evening, as twilight turned to darkness, General Sturgis, commanding all the forces of the fatal expedition, arrived on horseback at the rear of the retreating column. The men of the Ninth watched with bitterness as General Sturgis and his officers passed around a bottle of whiskey. Then they galloped off, leaving Colonel Wilkin and his force alone to protect the retreat. But Wilkin continued to lead the troops defending the rear of the retreat, giving every inch of ground grudgingly, imploring his men to "keep on" resisting the rebel attack.

After two days and one night of steady retreat from the advancing rebels, Wilkin stopped his men Sunday night and ordered them to get some sleep. On Monday morning, June 12, the men awoke to another sweltering day. Because of the heat and slogging through mud and bogs, the shoes of the men came apart like paper. They covered their blistered feet with cloth cut away from their pants and continued the retreat for a third day.

Finally, on the fourth day of the retreat, a train from Memphis arrived with fresh reinforcements. At the first sight of relief, many of the men broke down and cried. But once they were safely back in Memphis, the men of the Ninth had only a few days to recover from the exhaustion of their retreat before they joined a new expedition, with Colonel Wilkin as one of the commanders, headed south again to battle the rebel troops.

The Union forces made camp on a small hill with a growth of timber just north of Tupelo, Mississippi.

On the morning of July 14, 1864, facing an open plain, Union forces deployed in two lines of infantry in front and one line behind. Ammunition boxes were distributed along the lines. Artillery was positioned to rake the open field across which the rebels planned to attack with the expectation of the same victory they had achieved at Brice's Crossroads.

By noon, it was another sultry, thick Mississippi day. A determined rebel force of nine thousand men, again led by General Nathan Bedford Forrest, attacked at midafternoon across the open field. This time, Forrest's tactical genius was no match for the Union Army's superior position. After three hours of fierce exchanges of musket fire, the rebels withdrew, leaving their dead piled in heaps on the open field.

But the rebels attacked again immediately. Colonel Wilkin galloped forward on his mount to again encourage his troops at the battle line. The fight was all-out, with the mayhem of musket fire, battle cries, war whoops, and the deep boom of cannon fire. The action was everything Colonel Wilkin had been eager to return to since the Battle of Bull Run. But he did not even have time to dismount and join his troops before a minié ball cracked into his head. He fell to the ground, killed instantly.

In his death the tiny soldier who had courted danger distinguished himself as the highest-ranking Minnesota officer killed in the Civil War. He had spent almost a year in Missouri, hearing of glorious battles like Gettysburg from afar, hoping to get his own troops into a good fight. Instead, they had only guarded bridges and chased down ragtag bands of Missouri bushwhackers. The only event of consequence—and it had turned out to be so controversial that the U.S. Senate had ordered an investigation of it—had been the incident at the Otterville station. Now, his stubbornness in retreat had won the love of his men. He was, they said, fearless. But in his last letters to his family in Minnesota, he confessed that the sound of cannon fire on the battlefield was frightening. He remained committed to "proficiency in drill" as a condition of battlefield success. Even in retreat, he expected men to march in "cadence." Despite the panic and confusion that was everywhere, he said his own troops had retreated from Brice's Crossroad "slowly and in fine order."

Private James Woodbury was not among those men who made their escape in "fine order" from Brice's Crossroads. In the panic of the retreat, he and hundreds of other men decided to leave the clog of soldiers moving slowly north along the narrow, muddy road. Their intention was to find shelter in the surrounding woods, where they would sleep by day and continue their escape at night.

The decision was a fatal one, and Woodbury was captured along with 259 men of the Ninth Minnesota that first day of retreat. Before June was over, he was sent to the infamous Confederate prisoner-of-war camp in Andersonville, Georgia. Twenty-six thousand Union soldiers were jammed into a stockade meant for ten thousand. With grim humor, the men confined at Andersonville joked that if they weren't actually in hell, it was only a short march to it. Open pits functioned as latrines. A sea of crude tents fashioned from uniforms was meant to be protection against the hot Georgia sun. But the makeshift tents only served as kilns that cooked the prisoners. Others dug holes in the ground that turned into muddy pigsties when it rained. Thieves and thugs roamed among the prisoners like pack dogs. Hungry and thirsty, the prisoners dug their own wells in a desperate attempt to find uncontaminated water.

Andersonville was a pestilential netherworld for the condemned. The captured soldiers came down with diarrhea, dysentery, gangrene, and scurvy. They coughed and choked and spit and suffered "shake" and then died—nine hundred men a month. For Private James Woodbury the horror of Andersonville after the solitude and beauty of prairie life was unbearable. On July 27, 1864, he was admitted to the Andersonville hospital with chronic diarrhea. The hospital was a series of tented wards in an enclosed field south of the stockade. Removal from the misery of the stockade should have been cause for relief, but it meant all the more horror. There was no bedding in the hospital, no clothing, no bandages, and the only sedation was turpentine. The fractures and limb stumps of wounded prisoners swarmed with maggots. Patients complained that they were being eaten by worms.

Woodbury spiked a fever; his head throbbed; his stomach cramped. He cried out for water. But he began to dry out and shrink, as if he were a carcass baking in the hot sun. His skin wrinkled, and his bones stood out like brittle sticks. He began breathing in intermittent gulps, as if he were biting the air. His eyes turned milky, and he sank into a coma. Finally, on the afternoon of August 2, 1864, in the presence of at least thirty other moaning patients who died that day, his heart stopped.

He died without knowing that back in Minnesota, just weeks earlier, his wife Amanda had delivered their first child. Meanwhile, she could not accept the reality that her James was dead. He had been a loving, kind husband. He would have been just as loving and kind a father. His letters to her and his family had been filled with sweet longing to return to Mower County. He missed the pleasures of maple syrup and the juicy tartness of a fresh apple. Mower County would soon be rich with plums and grapes. "If I had known as much about [the army] as I do now," he had written, "I would never have enlisted." But he had volunteered for duty and then fallen into a bitter mood of regret. That regret had led him to avoid the predicament of those soldiers who had volunteered to rescue the slaves at the Otterville station. He had escaped the imprisonment and the threat of death those men faced. While they had suffered in the Jefferson City prison, he dreamt of being back in Mower County soon. He and Amanda would enjoy the prairie wildflowers and the meadowlarks. They would sit together in the evening stillness of their dooryard and watch the sun set. Even the cold winters would be an opportunity for cozy refuge. But he had died without realizing his dreams, "alone and uncared for."

His body was tagged with a paper ticket identifying name, rank, and regiment; and he was dragged out of the Andersonville hospital to a dirt road, where he was stacked in a mule-drawn wagon, then hauled to the prison cemetery three hundred yards north of the camp. The cemetery was called a "bivouac for the dead." The burial trenches were five feet deep and long enough to contain one thousand men laid side by side, without coffins, shrouds, or ceremonies. A simple wood stake with only a number marked the spot where Private James Woodbury, Ninth Minnesota, was buried.

In early August of 1865, the government published a two-hundred-page pamphlet that listed all of the Union dead. But the war was over, and those who had survived were coming home. Celebrations were in order. In Brooklyn ten thousand spectators watched a hotly contested baseball game. A huge crowd turned out to watch the horse races at Saratoga Race Course, and the women were described in the *New York Times* as a "galaxy of beauty and fashion." Long-exiled refugees were returning to their home states to resume wholesome living, free of the mud and gunshots and bloody fields of war.

For weeks late that summer, steamers had been working their way up the Mississippi with various Minnesota regiments returning from the war, heading for St. Paul and Fort Snelling, where the soldiers would be mustered out. There were banquets and celebrations, and one woman vowed to kiss every returning boy.

On Friday, August 11, it was the Ninth Minnesota's turn to return by steamboat to glory. At each landing—Winona, Wabasha, Red Wing—citizens lined the river banks and waved and cheered. Bands played on shore. There were red, white, and blue banners flying from the trees. There were cannon salutes that echoed up and down the river valley. At each landing, citizens presented the soldiers with home-baked food. When they reached St. Paul, they were greeted by two thousand cheering citizens and escorted to the state capitol and welcomed home.

But those enlisted men—minus the 119 who, like James Woodbury, had died in the Andersonville prison—were battle scarred and sickly. They had infected wounds, hearing loss, and chronic diarrhea. Some were still so stunned by the din and bedlam of war that their only words were a rambling mix-up of battlefields and commanders, with only the logic of a nightmare.

Among those few who disembarked at Fort Snelling without a scratch was Corporal Henry Ehmke. After the incident at the Otterville station and after his release from the Jefferson City prison, he had escaped capture during the retreat from Brice's Crossroads and then fought bravely at Tupelo, Memphis, and Nashville. The government apparently thought less of his bravery than of his equipment losses during the campaigns, and even though he still had not received his enlistment bounty, they deducted thirty-four cents from his pay for lost equipment.

Ehmke had marched fifteen hundred miles from one battlefield to another, to the point where he hardly knew or cared where he was. It would be just another battlefield on which he stood a good chance of dying. He had endured hunger and hospitalization with dysentery. Those long marches and confinement to a hospital bed had made him even more spindly than he had been at enlistment. But back at Minnesota's Fort Snelling, he enjoyed the pleasure of good food and "indolent" soldiering while he rebuilt his strength.

He was mustered out in late August. The nomad who had traveled the world by steamboat and rail and riverboat and finally by shank's mare across Missouri and down to Mississippi and into Tennessee and Kentucky was now determined to take up married life and settle down.

He and his new bride from Winona moved up out of the river valley and took up farming ten miles outside the town. The long hours of hard work proved not to be the realization of Ehmke's settlement dreams, and he and his wife soon moved back to Winona, where he opened a butcher shop. After a few years what little was left of his restless temperament asserted itself for a final time, and he went to work for a Winona milling company as a weigh master.

He was the good soldier who had fought against Sioux Indians without injury. He had faced being shot during the release of the slaves at the Otterville station. He had escaped bullets and howling rebels during the retreat from Brice's Crossroads. He had survived cannon shrapnel and even bayonet charges without so much as a trickle of blood. But one day at work in the elevator of the Winona flour mill, he slipped and fell into a milling machine and had his foot torn off.

He was given disability retirement and continued to

live for years in Winona. To newcomers he was the cragged Civil War veteran with the bristly beard who must have been shot in battle and now hobbled around with a wooden foot. He died in 1929 at age eighty-eight. His obituary made mention of his participation in the Civil War battle at Tupelo but not the incident at the Otterville station. He was buried in Winona, the last stop in the world for the string bean nomad.

After his release from the Jefferson City prison, Sergeant Francis Merchant, the Otterville "ringleader," spent two months in the hospital, sickish and bilious from confinement. As soon as he was released, he rejoined the Ninth Regiment and was part of the force that held back the rebels during the retreat from Brice's Crossroads.

In December of 1864 he and the Ninth Regiment joined a huge expedition of Union forces sent to defend Nashville from rebel attack. In rain and mud and fog the regiment encamped south of Nashville and threw up a breastwork of stone and dirt that curled through the rolling hillside like the Great Wall. Then early in the morning of December 15, 1864, the men leaped the breastwork and charged Confederate forces waiting for the fog to lift. Merchant and his fellow soldiers shouted "Minnesota! Minnesota!" as they darted through stumps and fallen trees with fixed bayonets.

The earth shook from artillery fire and musket volleys; and before Merchant reached the enemy's line, a minié ball struck his hand and shattered the bones. The injury did not stop him during the battle. And after a decisive Union victory, his wounded hand slowly healed, and he resumed his climb up the ranks. He was commissioned a first lieutenant and took command of Company C from Mower County. Shortly before his discharge in August of 1865, he was promoted once more, this time to captain.

Immediately after the war, Merchant married and returned to his farm west of Austin and again took up the hard work of farming his quarter section of land in the middle of that "perfect paradise of flowers." In 1880 on Decoration Day, which would eventually become Memorial Day, Merchant joined the crowd of citizens and veterans in Austin who listened to a moving speech by a town clergyman who praised the Union veterans. "The world had never seen such an army," he said. The war had been initiated to save the Union, but it had also "blotted out our greatest national disgrace, the crime of human slavery." Fifty soldiers from Austin had gone to war. A dozen had been killed. They were all "honest men, good citizens, kind husbands and neighbors."

On the basis of that praise, which Francis Merchant deserved as much as any of the Mower County veterans, he soon found himself as the chief of police in the town of Albert Lea, Minnesota, west of Austin. He was, the Albert Lea newspapers wrote, "made of sound sense."

By 1888 his Civil War heroism and his leadership at the Otterville station were forgotten, and political opponents charged him with being "inefficient, incompetent, and evil." And they had him arrested. His arrest was as unjust as his imprisonment had been in Jefferson City. Friends signed petitions on his behalf as chief of police. Despite the petitions, he submitted a letter of resignation. He was not yet fifty. He had no work, his wounded hand often pained him, and he suffered chronic kidney disease that affected his feet and slowed his walk. His friends gave him an ebony cane with a gold head. Those same friends raised one hundred dollars as a gift to him to tide his family over.

He moved to Minneapolis and took a position in a lumberyard with old friends from the Ninth Regiment. By 1890 there were only fifty survivors of the original force of one thousand men of the Ninth Minnesota. Still respected by his fellow soldiers, Merchant served as president for the loosely organized, aging clutch of Civil War veterans.

By 1911 he had already lost two of his children when his wife of forty-six years died. He moved to Oakland, California, to live with one of his sons. On Sunday, October 1, 1927, on a warm, still day in Oakland, he died at eighty-five years old, the oldest surviving member of the Ninth Minnesota, Company C.

The following day the slugger Babe Ruth hit his sixtieth home run of the season. He had broken his own record of fifty-nine home runs, set six years earlier. Newspapers throughout the country recounted Ruth's baseball feats, which included 416 career home runs. In the nationwide celebration for such prodigious athletic feats, there was little notice of the death of Francis Merchant, who for ten minutes at a remote train station in frontier Missouri had bravely led a small group of Minnesota soldiers in a clash over slavery. Measured against Gettysburg and Vicksburg and Appomattox, it was too small a step in the battle to preserve the Union and end slavery to be long remembered.

Francis Merchant's body was returned to Austin, Minnesota, where he was buried in a family plot in a town cemetery. Surrounded by small tombstones that stuck up like teeth, there was no marker laid for his grave. Decades later gravediggers pointed to the unmarked gravesite and sought to account for how such a heroic figure could come to such an inglorious end. "There's a lot of 'em from those days," the gravediggers said, "buried like that."

Missouri slave owner Charles Walker did not submit a report to Secretary of War Stanton on the incident at the Otterville station. After the incident, he continued to farm in Pettis County. He had a respectable and promising family. He knew that the days of slavery in Missouri were numbered. That realization was what had prompted him to try to ship his slaves to Kentucky to sell them. But the release of his slaves by the Minnesota soldiers had left him without field hands. So he hired and boarded white and black help. The black men were no longer slaves but paid laborers who worked his fields and broke his hemp alongside the white laborers.

Despite orders to local authorities to keep track of freed slaves, there was no record of what happened to John and his family. To make sure that freed slaves did not disappear into a post–Civil War sinkhole of poverty and despair, a Freedman's Relief Bureau was formed to aid former slaves, but newspaper editors complained that their meetings to plot strategies were nothing but "speechifying." Emancipated slaves and fugitives like John and his family were left mostly to their own escape devices. Their choices were few.

They could have hidden out in the Otterville woods. But there were still bushwhackers in Missouri who were as "fierce on the track of fugitives" as bloodhounds. Justices of the peace could issue warrants for "crafty and cunning" runaways who were "lurking in swamps and woods." John and his family could have been tracked down and caught, then sold back into slavery in Kentucky. "My god," the victims of recapture and continued slavery cried, "how long are we going to be cursed with this mockery?" For John and his family, it would have been the very fate they had tried to avoid.

Some argued that the freed slaves would make good soldiers. They should be armed, "and in God's name bid him strike for the human race." Nearly 200,000 freed slaves and fugitives, nearly 4,000 of them from Missouri, fought bravely alongside Union forces. So John could have entered the army and received protection; but with the official confusion over what was to be done with fugitive slaves, there was the risk that military officials would return them to their owners. Or they could be captured by Confederate troops and treated not as prisoners of war but as property deserving of death. Rebel sympathizers in Missouri said the whole business of enrolling Negroes in the Union Army was a "damn abolitionist scheme!" Confederate editors wrote that Yankees drove black men, like so many cattle, to be enlisted in the Union Army. Meanwhile, those same Confederate editors insisted that free Negroes could be made to serve in the rebel army. "We have a right to do what we please with our slaves," they said.

Or John and his family could have fled to freedom. They could have slept in barns by day and traveled mostly by foot or wagon at night, eating raw corn and potatoes. They could have worked their way west from Otterville, back along the same route that John had taken to make his exhausting run for help. They could have reached western Missouri, then turned north to Iowa, resting in a safe farmhouse with secret rooms, then moving north and east across Iowa, Illinois, Michigan, until they reached Canada.

Wherever John and his family went, the fate of the one man who had triggered the incident at the Otterville station remains a mystery. He and his family disappeared into the Otterville woods like frightened ghosts and vanished into history.

# Notes

## 1. The Great Emancipator

1 **the Great Russian Ball**: "The Great Russian Ball," *Harper's Weekly*, November 21, 1863, 746; and Jon Carroll, *San Francisco Chronicle*, October 15, 1999, C-20.

1 **a brief one**: Michael Fellman, *Inside War: The Guerilla Conflict in Missouri during the American Civil War* (New York: Oxford University Press, 1989), 23.

2 **"If slavery is not wrong, nothing is wrong"**: James McPherson, *Antietam: The Battle That Changed the Course of the Civil War* (New York: Oxford University Press, 2002), 61–62.

2 **Ninety thousand men**: James McPherson, *Tried by War: Abraham Lincoln as Commander in Chief* (New York: Penguin Group, 2008), 25.

2 **Antietam**: McPherson, *Antietam*, 116–31, 134.

2 **"At no time"**: McPherson, *Antietam*, 135.

2 **"a strange and terrible battle"**: Bruce Catton, *Never Call Retreat* (New York: Doubleday, 1965), 12.

2 **"a masterly piece of butchery . . . with not a thing accomplished"**: Gary Gallagher, *The American Civil War: The War in the East 1861–May 1863* (Oxford: Osprey Publishing, 2001), 63.

2 **Chancellorsville**: McPherson, *Tried by War*, 639–45.

2 **Gettysburg**: Gallagher, *American Civil War*, 9–10.

3 **a thousand champagne corks**: *Harper's Weekly*, November 21, 1863, 746; and Jon Carroll, *San Francisco Chronicle*, October 15, 1999, C-20.

3 **gathered his thirteen sleepy slaves**: "Mower County Boys in Prison in Jefferson City, Missouri," *Saint Paul Pioneer Weekly*, December 10, 1863; S. Exec. Doc. No. 38-24, at 2 (1864) (*Congressional Serial Set*, vol. 1176) (hereafter referred to as "SED 24"); and Diane Mutti Burke, *On Slavery's Border: Missouri's Small-Slaveholding Households, 1815–1865* (Athens: University of Georgia Press, 2010), 227.

3  **shipping them by train:** "Mower County Boys in Prison"; SED 24, at 2; and Harrison Trexler, *Slavery in Missouri* (Baltimore: Johns Hopkins Press, 1914), 91–97.

3  **Walker often worked the fields of his farm:** Burke, *On Slavery's Border*, 4, 8, 9, 102, 160; and Aaron Astor, *Rebels on the Border: Civil War, Emancipation, and the Reconstruction of Kentucky and Missouri* (Baton Rouge: Louisiana State University Press, 2012), 68–69.

3  **going on for decades:** Ira Berlin, Barbara Fields, Thavolia Glymph, Joseph Reidy, Leslie Rowland, *Freedom: A Documentary History of Emancipation, 1861–1867*, ser. 1, vol. 1, *The Destruction of Slavery* (Cambridge: Cambridge University Press, 1985), 110, 135, 140; Burke, *On Slavery's Border*, 178, 286, 295; James McPherson, *Battle Cry of Freedom: The Civil War Era* (Oxford: Oxford University Press, 1988), 78, 85; Astor, *Rebels on the Border*, 73; and *Wikipedia*, s.v. "Quantrill's Raiders," accessed May 9, 2012, http://en.wikipedia.org/wiki/Quantrill's_Raiders.

3  **underground railroad:** *Wikipedia*, s.v. "underground railroad," accessed June 10, 2011, http://en.wikipedia.org/wiki/Underground_Railroad; and McPherson, *Battle Cry*, 79–80, 83, 85.

4  **Yankee safety would mean neglect and abuse:** Berlin et al., *Freedom*, 110.

4  **corn cutters and clubs:** McPherson, *Battle Cry*, 85.

4  **On the East Coast:** Berlin et al., *Freedom*, 62, 84, 98, 105, 116, 122, 135, 190.

4  **"stampede to the enemy":** Burke, *On Slavery's Border*, 284, 295; and Astor, *Rebels on the Border*, 107.

4  **battleground on a smaller scale:** "The Seat of the War in Missouri," *New York Times*, October 5, 1861; "The War in the West," *New York Times*, November 3, 1961; MacDonald Demuth, *The History of Pettis County* (New York: Printer, 1882), 43; and Clement Evans, ed., *Confederate Military History*, vol. 9, *Kentucky and Missouri* (Syracuse: Blue and Grey Press), 10, 16, 20, 32–33.

4  **The Missouri Compromise of 1820:** Doris Goodwin, *Team of Rivals: The Political Genius of Abraham Lincoln* (New York: Simon and Schuster, 2005), 61; and Gallagher, *American Civil War*, 14.

5  **split Missouri into bitter factions:** Carolyn Bartels, *The Civil War in Missouri Day by Day, 1861–1865* (Independence MO: Two Trails Publishing, 1992), 8, 25; Fellman, *Inside War*, 65, 397; William Parrish, *A History of Missouri*, vol. 3, *1860–1875* (Columbia: University of Missouri Press, 1973), 1–29; and Burke, *On Slavery's Border*, 272–73.

5  **"sisterhood":** Astor, *Rebels on the Border*, 63.

5 Missouri state guard: Astor, *Rebels on the Border*, 11, 75, 80–81, 90, 261, 269; Parrish, *History of Missouri*, 18; and Bartels, *Civil War in Missouri*, 2.

5 "Throw off the yoke of the North": Bartels, *Civil War in Missouri*, 42.

5 a state convention of politicians: Parrish, *History of Missouri*, 10–11.

5 refused the call: McPherson, *Tried by War*, 25; and Astor, *Rebels on the Border*, 78–79.

5 the character of the state had changed: Parrish, *History of Missouri*, 7–8; and Astor, *Rebels on the Border*, 19, 80, 144, 210, 272.

6 "Home Guard": Kirby Ross, "Federal Militia in Missouri," *Civil War St. Louis*, accessed May 18, 2012, civlwarstlouis.com/militia/federalmilitia.htm; and Astor, *Rebels on the Border*, 126.

6 Governor Jackson met secretly: Parrish, *History of Missouri*, 12–15.

6 various militia units: Astor, *Rebels on the Border*, 55, 80; McPherson, *Battle Cry*, 290; Ross, "Federal Militia in Missouri"; and Astor, *Rebels on the Border*, 142, 260.

6 "Camp Jackson": McPherson, *Battle Cry*, 290–91; Burke, *On Slavery's Border*, 270; and Astor, *Rebels on the Border*, 63.

6 fifty thousand young Missouri men: Bartels, *Civil War in Missouri*, 12.

6 government in exile: Bartels, *Civil War in Missouri*, 12; and Parrish, *History of Missouri*, 31, 51.

6 "utterly impossible": Parrish, *History of Missouri*, 33.

7 second exile: Parrish, *History of Missouri*, 25–26, 38, 45, 47.

7 hit-and-run tactics: Astor, *Rebels on the Border*, 90–91, 115, 117.

7 bulletproof iron plates: Parrish, *History of Missouri*, 27.

7 General John Fremont: Astor, *Rebels on the Border*, 107; Parrish, *History of Missouri*, 28–29, 66, 89; Bartels, *Civil War in Missouri*, 20; Berlin et al., *Freedom*, 30, 397–98; McPherson, *Tried by War*, 55; Catton, *Never Call Retreat*, 109; Fellman, *Inside War*, 65; and James Denny, "Civil War Entrenchment Near Otterville," *Boonslick Heritage* 7, no. 2 (June 1999): 3.

8 gradual and less antagonistic approach: Burke, *On Slavery's Border*, 266, 281, 285; and Berlin et al., *Freedom*, 22, 45, 53–54.

8 relieved him of his command: Berlin et al., *Freedom*, 397.

8 Little Dixie: Astor, *Rebels on the Border*, 12–13, 17–19, 21, 52–53, 79, 117; and Burke, *On Slavery's Border*, 12, 27, 51, 95.

8 backbone: Astor, *Rebels on the Border*, 12–13.

8 Southern: Astor, *Rebels on the Border*, 18; and Burke, *On Slavery's Border*, 333.

9 "white trash": Don Bowen, "Guerilla War in Western Missouri, 1862–1865: Historical Extensions of the Relative Deprivation Hypothesis," *Comparative Studies in Society and History* 19, no. 1 (January 1977): 30–32,

50; Fellman, *Inside War*, 23, 83, 110–11, 113, 126, 135, 137, 217; McPherson, *Tried by War*, 784, 786; and Goodwin, *Team of Rivals*, 183.

9 **Outlaws, bandits, and horse thieves**: Astor, *Rebels on the Border*, 90.

9 **psychopathic killers**: McPherson, *Battle Cry*, 785.

9 **not as trashy and villainous**: Bowen, "Guerila War in Western Missouri," 37–50; McPherson, *Tried by War*, 785; and Fellman, *Inside War*, 259.

9 **Francis Lieber**: *Wikipedia*, s.v. "Lieber Code," accessed March 28, 2011, http://en.wikipedia.org/wiki/Lieber_Code; and Fellman, *Inside War*, 83, 217.

10 **William Clarke Quantrill**: Parrish, *History of Missouri*, 61; and Bartels, *Civil War in Missouri*, 67.

10 **attack on Lawrence, Kansas**: Parrish, *History of Missouri*, 61, 101; McPherson, *Battle Cry*, 785–87; Fellman, *Inside War*, 24–25; and *Wikipedia*, s.v. "Quantrill's Raiders," accessed June 13, 2011, http://en.wikipedia.org/wiki/Quantrill%E2%80%99s_Raiders.

11 **General Order no. 11**: McPherson, *Tried by War*, 786; Burke, *On Slavery's Border*, 278; Astor, *Rebels on the Border*, 115; *Wikipedia*, s.v. "General Order No. 11 (1863)," accessed June 1, 2011, http://en.wikipedia.org/wiki/General_Order_No._11_(1863); Fellman, *Inside War*, 82–84, 86; and Parrish, *History of Missouri*, 101.

11 **recruit rebel soldiers**: Evans, 130.

11 **needed more troops**: Bartels, *Civil War in Missouri*, 42.

11 **institution of slavery in Missouri**: Trexler, *Slavery in Missouri*, 27; Harriet Frazier, *Slavery and Crime in Missouri, 1773–1865* (Jefferson: McFarland, 2001), 98, 166; and SED 24, at 3.

11 **His authorization to do so**: SED 24, at 4.

## 2. Charles W. Walker

12 **born in Casey County**: "James T. Walker (1795)," accessed August 26, 2009, walkercousins.com/wbibles/jamest.htm; "George-Sterling-Smith-L Archive," RootsWeb.com, accessed August 26, 2009, archiver.rootsweb.ancestry.com/th/read/George-Sterling-Smith/2004; "Tax Deeds Purchased, Volume 12," 944, Missouri State Archives, Land Patents: 1831–1996, Office of the Secretary of State, Jefferson City; Keith Daleen, e-mails to author, June 24–25, 2009; Parrish, *History of Missouri*, 38–44; U.S. Bureau of the Census, *Mt. Sterling Township, Pettis County Missouri* (Washington DC: Bureau of the Census, 1860), 72, Federal Archives and Research Center, San Bruno, California; Trexler, *Slavery in Missouri*, 46, 217; Melton McLaurin, *Celia, A Slave: A True Story* (Athens: University of Georgia Press, 1991), 35–36; U.S. Bureau of the Census, *Pettis County, Mis-*

*souri* (Washington DC: Bureau of the Census, 1850), 116B; Frazier, *Slavery and Crime in Missouri*, 98, 166; Demuth, *History of Pettis County*, 236, 343, 352, 404–8, 923–28; "Concerning the 9th Minnesota Regiment," *New York Times*, March 5, 1964; "Report of Secretary Stanton," *New York Times*, December 13, 1863; "Slaves in Missouri in 1860," *Howard County Advertiser*, January 19, 1903; and Burke, *On Slavery's Border*, 8, 49.

13  **The value of slaves began to decline:** Astor, *Rebels on the Border*, 104–5, 111.

13  **Pacific Railroad terminus in Sedalia:** Demuth, *History of Pettis County*, 371, 404–8; "The Katy Depot," accessed June 7, 2009, http://www.katydepotsedalia.com ; and "Bird's Eye View of the City of Sedalia," accessed March 3, 2010, http://www. loc.gov/item/73693491.

13  **two-mile ride into Sedalia:** Demuth, *History of Pettis County*, 52–56, 399, 447–51; and Pettis County EBooks, *Pettis County Missouri* (Higginsville MO: Hearthstone Legacy Publications, 2006), 408–10, 413.

14  **Union soldiers were stationed:** *Harper's Weekly*, July 12, 1862, 280.

14  **"No provost marshal":** SED 24, at 4; and Major General Schofield, "Special Orders 304," November 10, 1863, *Letters Received by the Secretary of War, Main Series, 1801–1879*, microcopy 221, roll 252, JPG 1017, headquarters, Department of Missouri, National Archives and Records Administration (hereafter NARA, *Letters Received*), College Park, Maryland.

14  **promptly wrote out a permit:** SED 24, at 4.

14  **Ives House:** "Bird's Eye View of Sedalia"; Demuth, *History of Pettis County*, 448; and *Missouri in 1861: The Civil War Letters of Francis B. Wilkie* (Iowa City: Press of the Camp Pope Bookshop, 2001), 4:255.

14  **two boxcars:** "Bird's Eye View of Sedalia"; and Lt. Col. Alan Koenig, *Mars Gets New Chariots: The Iron Horse in Combat, 1861–65* (New York: iUniverse, 2006), xxi.

14  **"Permission is granted":** NARA, *Letters Received*, JPG 1006.

15  **the names on the certificate:** SED 24, at 4; NARA, *Letters Received*, JPG 1006–8; U.S. Bureau of the Census, *Slave Schedule, 1860* (Washington DC: Bureau of the Census, 1860), Mt. Sterling Township, Missouri.

15  **several lawsuits pending:** Berlin et al., *Freedom*, 465–66.

16  **not to permit the shipment of slaves:** "Missouri War Items," *New York Times*, September 19, 1861; "Movements in Missouri," *New York Times*, September 24, 1861; "News of the Day," *New York Times*, October 5, 1861; and "Mower County Boys in Prison."

16  **"Pins, threads, combs, buttons!":** *Harper's Weekly*, July 19, 1862, 280.

17  **fifty thousand dollars of equity:** U.S. Bureau of the Census, *Pettis County, Missouri*, 116B.

17  **its first stop:** "Mower County Boys in Prison."

17 **Smithton had been the terminus:** SED 24, at 1; and Pettis County EBooks, *Pettis County Missouri*, 1011.

17 **made escape a possibility:** SED 24, at 4.

18 **John bolted:** SED 24, at 4; and Demuth, *History of Pettis County*, 923–27.

19 **bushwhackers and guerillas in the area:** Demuth, *History of Pettis County*, 343; and Charles Lothrop, *A History of the First Regiment Iowa Cavalry* (Lyons, Iowa: Beers and Eaton, 1890), 58–62.

19 **accused of murder and rape:** "Shocking Murder in Missouri," *New York Times*, July 27, 1853.

20 **make a run for Otterville:** SED 24, at 2.

20 **a small cantonment of Union troops:** SED 24, at 2.

21 **Little Dixie:** Astor, *Rebels on the Border*, 12–13, 17–19, 21, 52–53, 79, 117; and Burke, *On Slavery's Border*, 12, 27, 51, 95.

21 **cut and then break hemp:** [Wilson Bocine?] to Milton Thompson, July 11, 1844, Berry-Thompson-Walker Family Papers, 1830–93, Western Historical Manuscript Collection (hereafter WHMC), Columbia, Missouri; Burke, *On Slavery's Border*, 99–100, 131; and Astor, *Rebels on the Border*, 23, 254.

21 **he wasn't sure:** For a fit young man to run twenty miles in two hours would have been difficult but attainable: e-mail from Ron Etherton to author, June 5, 2011; and Christopher McDougall, *Born to Run* (New York: Vintage Books, 2009).

## 3. John

22 **John leaped off the platform:** SED 24, at 3–4.

22 **a field day:** Berlin et al., *Freedom*, 163.

22 **severe punishment:** Berlin et al., *Freedom*, 86–87, 267, 313, 321, 323, 348, 590; Burke, *On Slavery's Border*, 10, 82, 131, 145, 168, 172, 183, 194–95, 198, 261, 294–95; and Astor, *Rebels on the Border*, 69, 104, 118, 134, 180.

22 **ears cropped:** Astor, *Rebels on the Border*, 30.

22 **open prairie east of Sedalia:** Pettis County EBooks, *Pettis County Missouri*, 361, 374, 409; and Demuth, *History of Pettis County*, 923–27.

22 **woods encampments of bushwhackers:** Lothrop, *History of the First Regiment*, 58–62.

23 **They called it a "nigger crop":** James F. Hopkins, *A History of the Hemp Industry in Kentucky* (Lexington: University of Kentucky, 1941), 4, 24–30, 132–40, 196; and Burke, *On Slavery's Border*.

23 **The hard work of breaking the hemp:** Trexler, *Slavery in Missouri*, 23–24, 93; Lord Somerville, *A Treatise on Hemp* (London: J. Harding, 1808), 231–33; and Burke, *On Slavery's Border*, 99, 131.

23 **"Wanted to hire":** Trexler, *Slavery in Missouri*, 19.

24 **striking a compromise:** Frazier, *Slavery and Crime in Missouri*, 82–84; McLaurin, *Celia*, 14; Hasan Sesay, "A Brief History of the African American Experience" (unpublished manuscript, California State University at Chico History Department, n.d.), 36.

24 **provisions of the Constitution:** Trexler, *Slavery in Missouri*, 58, 135.

24 **"lawful and patriotic":** Harriet Beecher Stowe, *Uncle Tom's Cabin* (New York: Washington Square Press, 1962; originally published by John P. Jewett, 1852), 187.

24 **biblically sanctioned:** McLaurin, *Celia*, 60.

24 **Fugitive Slave Law:** Astor, *Rebels on the Border*, 185, 256; McPherson, *Battle Cry*, 78–81, 119–20; and *Wikipedia*, s.v. "Fugitive Slave Act of 1850," accessed January 3, 2010, http://en.wikipedia.org/wiki/Fugitive_Slave_Act_of_1850.

24 **"Negro thieves":** McLaurin, *Celia*, 62.

24 **clubbed to death the owner:** McLaurin, *Celia*, 33–34.

24 **mere property:** U.S. War Department, *The War of the Rebellion: A Compilation of the Official Records of the Union and Confederate Armies* (Washington DC: Government Printing Office, 1880–1901), ser. 2, vol. 1, 754, found online at Cornell University Library, Making of America Digital Collection (Ithaca NY: Cornell University Library), accessed June 19, 2009, http://ebooks.library.cornell.edu/m/moawar/waro.html (this collection is hereafter cited as Cornell, followed by the corresponding series and volume number).

24 **Abductions and escapes:** Trexler, *Slavery in Missouri*, 204; Berlin et al., *Freedom*, 1; and Douglas Larson, "Private Alfred Gales: From Slavery to Freedom," *Minnesota History Magazine* 57, no. 6 (2001): 277.

25 **Eliza:** Stowe, *Uncle Tom's Cabin*, 61.

25 **at any price:** Trexler, *Slavery in Missouri*, 204; and Berlin et al., *Freedom*, 509, 511, 592.

25 **"contraband":** Cornell, ser. 2, vol. 1, 754; and Larson, "Private Alfred Gales," 277.

25 **"to which they may be best adapted":** Cornell, ser. 2, vol. 1, 755; and Berlin et al., *Freedom*, 289–91.

25 **"I will never be voluntarily instrumental":** Cornell, ser. 2, vol. 1, 755.

25 **"no part of the duty of soldiers of the U.S.":** Berlin et al., *Freedom*, 14; and Cornell, ser. 2, vol. 1, 759.

25 **the property of these disloyals:** Cornell, ser. 2, vol. 1, 762.

25 **quickly stepped in:** Berlin et al., *Freedom*, 16–17, 415.

26 **"This is a war for the Union":** Cornell, ser. 2, vol. 1, 761.

26 **"discretion" was to be used:** Cornell, ser. 2, vol. 1, 803.

26 **abetting the enemy:** Cornell, ser. 2, vol. 1, 803.

26 **The governor of Missouri complained**: Berlin et al., *Freedom*, 419.

26 **"We are not here as nigger hunters"**: "Dodges of the Missouri Traitors," *New York Times*, January 14, 1862.

26 **even more ambiguities**: Cornell, ser. 2, vol. 1, 803; and W. F. Johnson, *History of Cooper County* (unpublished manuscript, 1919), 61, WHMC.

27 **The angry owner and his son**: Berlin et al., *Freedom*, 430.

27 **Emboldened by the army's protection**: Berlin et al., *Freedom*, 449.

27 **"There is a screw loose somewhere"**: Berlin et al., *Freedom*, 289–91, 434; Burke, *On Slavery's Border*, 285; and Astor, *Rebels on the Border*, 106–9.

27 **left to settle their affairs**: Lothrop, *History of the First Regiment*, 58–62; and Berlin et al., *Freedom*, 438, 461.

27 **"I can use no force"**: Cornell, ser. 2, vol. 1, 816.

27 **branded their slaves**: "Dodges of the Missouri Traitors."

28 **Emancipation Proclamation**: McPherson, *Battle Cry*, 563, 703.

28 **without labor to work their farms**: Berlin et al., *Freedom*, 451, 459.

28 **a haven for slave owners**: Berlin et al., *Freedom*, 493, 505, 569.

## 4. Sergeant Francis Merchant

31 **Otterville had been first settled**: Cooper County EBooks, *Cooper County Missouri* (Higginsville MO: Hearthstone Legacy Publications, 2004), 702, 705.

31 **"howling wilderness"**: Cooper County EBooks, *Cooper County Missouri*, 705, 708.

31 **"beanpoles and cornstalks"**: Francis Lord, *They Fought for the Union* (New York: Bonanza Books, 1960), 83; Demuth, *History of Pettis County*, 412–16; and "Movements in Missouri," *New York Times*, September 28, 1861.

31 **temporary terminus**: Cooper County EBooks, *Cooper County Missouri*, 707.

31 **"green bay tree"**: Cooper County EBooks, *Cooper County Missouri*, 707.

32 **"rose like magic"**: Cooper County EBooks, *Cooper County Missouri*, 707.

32 **grandest buildings**: Cooper County EBooks, *Cooper County Missouri*, 701, 707–8.

32 **Little Dixie**: Burke, *On Slavery's Border*, 12, 315–16.

32 **only twenty people**: Cooper County EBooks, *Cooper County Missouri*, 748.

32 **"items of curiosity"**: Cooper County EBooks, *Cooper County Missouri*, 748.

32 **crowded with immigrants**: Bartels, *Civil War in Missouri*, 60.

32 **secession convictions**: Denny, "Civil War Entrenchment," 8.

32 **"secesh ladies"**: Fellman, *Inside War*, 200–201.

32 high command of the Union: Denny, "Civil War Entrenchment," 2.

33 A company of German Home Guard: Trexler, *Slavery in Missouri*, 55; Cornell, ser. 2, vol. 1, 582; "Movements in Missouri"; "Missouri War Items"; Cooper County EBooks, *Cooper County Missouri*, 762; McPherson, *Antietam, Battle Cry*, 291; Fellman, *Inside War*, 10; Berlin et al., *Freedom*, 397; and Burke, *On Slavery's Border*, 276, 358.

33 "Employ as many men as you need": Denny, "Civil War Entrenchment," 2.

33 dug two deep trenches: Denny, "Civil War Entrenchment," 2, 4.

33 thirty-four soldiers died: Denny, "Civil War Entrenchment," 4.

33 three thousand Union troops: "News of the Day," *New York Times*, October 5, 1861; "The Rebellion," *New York Times*, October 8, 1861; Cornell, ser. 2, vol. 1, 820–21; and Lord, *They Fought for the Union*, 237.

33–34 log huts with wood floors: Lord, *They Fought for the Union*, 237.

34 kegs of powder explosives: Koenig, *Mars Gets New Chariots*, 76.

34 "Look out for bridge burners": Cornell, ser. 2, vol. 1, 238.

34 prevented the massing of troops: Denny, "Civil War Entrenchment," 3–4.

34 one small detachment of twenty-eight Union soldiers: Cornell, ser. 2, vol. 1, 535; and Denny, "Civil War Entrenchment," 4.

34 "Save it!": Cornell, ser. 1, vol. 22, 623, 626, 673.

34 October 9, 1863: Cooper County EBooks, *Cooper County Missouri*, 770; Bartels, *Civil War in Missouri*, 168, 170; Denny, "Civil War Entrenchment," 3, 5–6; Cornell, ser. 2, vol. 1, 238; Koenig, *Mars Gets New Chariots*, 76; "Newspaper Details," *New York Times*, October 16, 1863; Johnson, *History of Cooper County*, 57; Cornell, ser. 1, vol. 41, 741; and Cornell, ser. 1, vol. 22, 637.

35 "in a mass of seething, hissing fire": Cornell, ser. 1, vol. 22, 673; and Cooper County EBooks, *Cooper County Missouri*, 770.

35 the new bridge: Leon Basile, ed., "The Letters of a Minnesota Volunteer: The Correspondence of James M. Woodbury," *Lincoln Herald* 82 (1980): 441–42.

35 Colonel Alexander Wilkin: Ronald Hubbs, "The Civil War and Alexander Wilkin," *Minnesota History Magazine* 39 (Spring 1965): 173–76, 183; Adjutant General's Office, State of Minnesota, "Record of Minnesota Volunteers during the Rebellion, Final Records of Company 'C,'" *Report of the Adjutant General, Minnesota, December 15, 1866* (St. Paul MN: Pioneer Printing, 1866), 407, Minnesota State Historical Society, St. Paul MN (hereafter MSHS); and Joel Whitney Photograph Collection, MSHS.

35 "the crack regiment of the state": Hubbs, "Civil War and Alexander Wilkin," 183.

36 **Wilkin had pestered his superiors**: Col. Wilkin to Gen. Sibley, December 3, 14, 25, 1862, January 28, 1863, and April 5, 1863, U.S. Army, Minnesota Infantry Regiment, 9th, *Regimental Letters and Order Book, 9th Minnesota Infantry Regiment* (Washington DC: National Archives, 1961), MSHS (hereafter *Regimental Letters*).

36 **200,000 Union troops**: Lord, *They Fought for the Union*, 125.

36 **October 15, 1863**: Basile, "Letters of a Minnesota Volunteer," 441; Board of Commissioners, *Minnesota in the Civil and Indian Wars* (St. Paul: Pioneer Press, 1890), 419; "Letter from Missouri," *Winona Daily Republican*, November 6–7, 1863; Jack Coggins, *Arms and Equipment of the Civil War* (New York: Fairfax Press, 1983), 18–19, 111–14; and Cornell, ser. 1, vol. 22, 642.

36 **Settlers poured into Minnesota**: Mower County Historical Society (hereafter MCHS), *Mill on the Willow* (Austin MN: MCHS, 1984), 2; M. K. Armstrong, "Early History of Mower County," USGenWebArchives, accessed June 10, 2009, http://files.usgwarchives.org/mn/mower/newspapers/1863-66 .txt (site now discontinued), 9–21; and Harriet Torgrimson, "Of Days that Used to Be: History of Grand Meadow, Minnesota" (unpublished manuscript, courtesy of Jim Hanson, Grand Meadow MN), 4, 12, 25.

36 **wolves, rattlesnakes, long cold winters**: MCHS, *Mill on the Willow*, 2; Armstrong, "Early History of Mower County," 14; and Inter-State Historical Company, *History of Mower County, Minnesota: Together with Sketches of Its Towns, Villages, and Townships; Educational, Civil, Military, and Political Portraits of Prominent Persons, and Biographies of Representative Citizens; History of Minnesota, Embracing Accounts of the Prehistoric Races, and a Brief Review of Its Civil and Military History* (Mankato MN: Free Press Publishing, 1884), 321–58.

37 **"higher order of the wigwam"**: Inter-State Historical Company, *History of Mower County*, 9, 150, 192, 210, 213–14, 235; and "Just Received," *Minnesota Courier*, August 20, 1862.

37 **Great Barn**: MCHS, *Mill on the Willow*, 10; "The Early Years Were Exciting," *Austin Herald*, August 2, 1983; and "Ghost of 'Old Headquarters,'" *Mower County News*, January 28, 1926.

37 **read from the Constitution**: MCHS, *Mill on the Willow*, 3.

37 **a thousand men**: Historic Fort Snelling, "The Civil War (1861–1865)," Minnesota State Historical Society, accessed May 23, 2012, http://www .historicfortsnelling.org/history/military-history/civil-war.

37 **700,000 Union men**: "The American Civil War: Northern Draft of 1862," accessed May 22, 2012, http://www.etymonline.com/cw/draft .htm.

38 **300,000 men**: "American Civil War: Northern Draft of 1862."

38 **"old flag"**: "American Civil War: Northern Draft of 1862."

38 **"Come one, come all"**: "American Civil War: Northern Draft of 1862."

38 **volunteer quotas**: Inter-State Historical Company, *History of Mower County*, 601; Walter Trenerry, "The Minnesota Rebellion Act of 1862: A Legal Dilemma of the Civil War," *Minnesota History Magazine* 35, no. 1 (1956): 2; "War Meeting" *Minnesota Courier*, August 20, 1862; and "General Headquarters, State of Minnesota," *Minnesota Courier*, July 23, August 13, and August 20, 1862; Franklin Curtis-Wedge, *History of Winona County, Minnesota* (Chicago: H. C. Cooper, 1913), 382; and "American Civil War: Northern Draft of 1862."

38 **Volunteers came forward slowly**: "American Civil War: Northern Draft of 1862."

38 **Federal Militia Act**: McPherson, *Battle Cry*, 491–92, 600–601, 605, 608–9, 684, 758; "American Civil War: Northern Draft of 1862."; Historic Fort Snelling, "The Civil War (1861–1865)"; "Conscription (Military Draft) in the Civil War," Shotgun's Home of the American Civil War, accessed May 22, 2012, http://www.civilwarhome.com/conscription.htm; U-S-History.com, "American History: The Draft in the Civil War," Online Highways, accessed May 22, 2012, http://www.u-s-history.com; Leslie Harris, "The New York City Draft Riots of 1863," in *In the Shadow of Slavery: African Americans in New York City, 1626–1863* (Chicago: University of Chicago Press, 2003), excerpt found online at press.uchicago.edu/Misc/Chicago/317749 (accessed May 22, 2012); Benjamin Thomas and Harold Hyman, *Stanton: The Life and Times of Lincoln's Secretary of War* (New York: Knopf, 1962); and Gallagher, *American Civil War*, 9, 10, 22, 69.

38 **"about nine feet long"**: "American Civil War: Northern Draft of 1862."

38 **states took control**: "American Civil War: Northern Draft of 1862."

38 **"jury wheel"**: "American Civil War: Northern Draft of 1862."

38 **one hundred–dollar federal bounty**: "American Civil War: Northern Draft of 1862."

39 **"Volunteer and receive bounties"**: "American Civil War: Northern Draft of 1862."

39 **Thousands now offered**: "American Civil War: Northern Draft of 1862."

39 **"beneath the shadow"**: Trenerry, "Minnesota Rebellion Act," 2.

39 **cash supplement**: "War Meeting," "Proclamation," "General Headquarters, State of Minnesota," *Minnesota Courier*, August 20, 1862; Inter-State Historical Company, *History of Mower County*, 185; and Lord, *They Fought for the Union*, 4.

39 **hundreds of prairie settlers**: Kenneth Carley, *The Sioux Uprising of 1862* (St. Paul: MSHS, 1961), 28–31.

39 **Hastily assembled militia men**: "War Meeting in Austin," *Minnesota Courier*, July 23, 1862; and "General Headquarters, State of Minnesota."

39 **posted sentinels**: "The Early Years Were Exciting," *Austin Herald*, August 2, 1983.

39 **"Can not get out"**: "Man's Body in Tree since 1862 Found in 1919," *LeRoy Independent*, July 13, 2006.

40 **"Patriotic Mass Meeting"**: Inter-State Historical Company, *History of Mower County*, 214; "Old Headquarters," *Austin Daily Herald*, August 3, 1935; "War Meeting," *Minnesota Courier*, August 6, 13, 1862; MCHS, *Mill on the Willow*, 3; and Lord, *They Fought for the Union*, 12.

40 **"Who does not burn with a desire?"**: "The Duty of the Hour," *Minnesota Courier*, August 20, 1862.

40 **as young as eighteen**: Board of Commissioners, *Minnesota in the Civil and Indian Wars*, 443, 453.

40 **Francis Merchant**: Union Army, "Military Service Records—Francis Merchant," NARA, College Park, Maryland; Freeborn County Minnesota AHGP, "'History of Freeborn County,' 1882: Oakland Twp. Biographies," RootsWeb.com, accessed August 29, 2009, http://www.rootsweb.ancestry.com/~mnfreeb2/biographies/18820akland.html; "Mrs. Francis Merchant," *Mower County Transcript*, December 20, 1911; "Francis Merchant, 85," *Austin Daily Herald*, October 24, 1927; and Joel Whitney Photograph Collection, MSHS.

41 **"perfect paradise of flowers"**: Inter-State Historical Company, *History of Mower County*, 9.

41 **A hunting party from St. Paul**: MCHS, *Mill on the Willow*, 6.

41 **two Negro fugitives from Missouri**: MCHS, *Mill on the Willow*, 14.

## 5. Private Henry Ehmke

43 **Henry Ehmke**: "Henry Ehmke, Civil War Veteran," *Winona Republican-Herald*, March 11, 1929; Union Army, "Military Service Records—Henry Ehmke," NARA, College Park, Maryland; and Adjutant General's Office, *Report of the Adjutant General*, 449.

43 **A boisterous river town**: Winona County Historical Society, *River Town Winona: Its History and Architecture* (1979; repr., Winona MN: Winona County Historical Society, 2006), iv, v, 1–5, 7, 10–11; and Sharon Erickson Ropes and Jim Heinlen, *Primarily Prints: Celebrate 2000 with a Half-Century of Jim Heinlen* (Winona MN: Sugar Loaf Press, 1999), 11, 16.

44 **watch the paddle wheelers arrive**: Winona County Historical Society, *River Town Winona*, 10.

44 **"Boots, Shoes"**: Winona County Historical Society, *River Town Winona*, 4.

44 **"weightier than local chemistries"**: Erickson Ropes and Heinlen, *Primarily Prints*, 19; and Winona County Historical Society, *River Town Winona*, 4.

44 **German-language newspapers**: Cornell, ser. 1, vol. 22, 547–50.

45 **Winona would form a full company**: Board of Commissioners, *Minnesota in the Civil and Indian Wars*, 453–54; and Jerry Anderson, "Ninth Regiment Volunteer Infantry" (list, courtesy of Jerry Anderson).

45 **Cheering crowds**: "Camp near Jefferson City," *Mower County Register*, October 29, 1863.

45 **"solid column of bayonets and cannon"**: Inter-State Historical Company, *History of Mower County*, 186; "Sermon of Rev. C. E. Wright," *Mower County Transcript*, June 17, 1880.

45 **an official "mustering day"**: Lord, *They Fought for the Union*, 14; and Jim Anderson, e-mail to author, September 4, 2009.

46 **"Who would not gladly have the honor"**: "Reasons for Drafting," *Minnesota Courier*, August 20, 1862.

46 **regiment's first duty**: Board of Commissioners, *Minnesota in the Civil and Indian Wars*, 416–18.

46 **St. Peter, Minnesota**: Board of Commissioners, *Minnesota in the Civil and Indian Wars*, 416–17; and Col. Wilkin to Gen. Sibley, December 3, 14, 25, 1862, January 28, 1863, and April 5, 1863, in *Regimental Letters*.

46 **moved to Mankato**: Board of Commissioners, *Minnesota in the Civil and Indian Wars*, 418; and Hubbs, "Civil War and Alexander Wilkin," 3–4, 18.

46 **posted at Fort Ridgely**: Board of Commissioners, *Minnesota in the Civil and Indian Wars*, 416; and Basile, "Letters of a Minnesota Volunteer," 439–40.

47 **disrespectful remarks**: Wilkin to Sibley, April 5, 1863, in *Regimental Letters*.

47 **enrolled into the Union Army**: Board of Commissioners, *Minnesota in the Civil and Indian Wars*, 416–17; Jim Anderson, e-mail to author, September 4, 2009; and NARA, *Letters Received*, JPG 1163.

47 **served a sumptuous meal**: Board of Commissioners, *Minnesota in the Civil and Indian Wars*, 417; MCHS, *Mill on the Willow*, 3, 13; Basile, "Letters of a Minnesota Volunteer," 442; and "Dear Editor," *Mower County Register*, October 29, 1863.

48 **October 12, 1863**: Adjutant General's Office, *Report of the Adjutant General*, 66, 451; Basile, "Letters of a Minnesota Volunteer," 441–42; Board of Commissioners, *Minnesota in the Civil and Indian Wars*, 418; "Dear Editor"; and Cornell, ser. 1, vol. 22, 639.

48 **red clover**: journal entry, October 14, 1863, John Aiton and Family Papers, MSHS.

48 **raining and cold:** "Letter from Missouri," *Winona Daily Republican*, November 6–7, 1863.

49 **his warm but smoky tent:** Basile, "Letters of a Minnesota Volunteer," 389, 441; Board of Commissioners, *Minnesota in the Civil and Indian Wars*, 419; Hubbs, "Civil War and Alexander Wilkin," 185; Lord, *They Fought for the Union*, 125, 150; and Wilkin to Adjutant General, November 6, 1863, in *Regimental Letters*.

49 **guarding the Lamine Bridge:** Basile, "Letters of a Minnesota Volunteer," 441; Board of Commissioners, *Minnesota in the Civil and Indian Wars*, 419; "Letter from Missouri" *Winona Daily Republican*, November 6–7, 1863; Coggins, *Arms and Equipment*, 18–19, 111–14; Lord, *They Fought for the Union*, 262; and Astor, *Rebels on the Border*, 115.

49 **David Wellman of Winona:** Board of Commissioners, *Minnesota in the Civil and Indian Wars*, 416–18; Adjutant General's Office, *Report of the Adjutant General*, 448; Union Army, "Military Service Records—D. W. Wellman," NARA, College Park, Maryland; and Joel Whitney Photograph Collection, MSHS.

49 **"abandoned" his business:** Union Army, "Military Service Records—D. W. Wellman."

51 **"Whatever you did, you would be shot":** Lord, *They Fought for the Union*, 238.

## 6. Private James Woodbury

52 **octagonal blockhouse:** Lord, *They Fought for the Union*, 83.

52 **"Where is your commander?":** SED 24, at 3; Berlin et al., *Freedom*, 12, 13, 28; Lord, *They Fought for the Union*, 119; Cornell, ser. 1, vol. 28, 417; and Coggins, *Arms and Equipment*, 122.

53 **"My owner is an officer in the rebel army":** SED 24, at 4; Berlin et al., *Freedom*, 403, 468; "Mower County Boys in Prison"; Burke, *On Slavery's Border*, 285; and Astor, *Rebels on the Border*, 107.

53 **"He was shot four times":** SED 24, at 4.

54 **"please save my family":** Board of Commissioners, *Minnesota in the 54 and Indian Wars*, 419; and "Mower County Boys in Prison."

54 **the nearby tent of Marcus Whitman:** SED 24, at 3.

54 **"A big Negro came into camp":** SED 24, at 3.

55 **"Captain Wellman wishes the boys to volunteer":** SED 24, at 3; and "From the Ninth Regiment," *Mower County Register*, December 17, 1863.

55 **confusing orders:** Burke, *On Slavery's Border*, 285; Astor, *Rebels on the Border*, 107; General John Pope, "Notice," January 28, 1862, Headquarters District of Central Missouri; and Cornell, ser. 1, vol. 22.

56 **sacred as well as their military duty:** McPherson, *Battle Cry*, 119–20.

56 **moral blessing:** McPherson, *Battle Cry*, 56.

56 **"mudsill":** McPherson, *Battle Cry*, 196–98.

56 **"delivered up":** McPherson, *Battle Cry*, 52, 57, 78–79, 81, 83, 88.

57 **"Talk, talk, talk!":** McPherson, *Battle Cry*, 201–6.

57 **two Confiscation Acts:** McPherson, *Battle Cry*, 80, 88–89, 353 355, 356, 498–99; McPherson, *Tried by War*, 107; Berlin et al., *Freedom*, 16–18, 30, 441; Gallagher, *American Civil War*, 64; Fellman, *Inside War*, 212–13; Catton, *Never Call Retreat*, 111; Burke, *On Slavery's Border*, 164, 285; and Astor, *Rebels on the Border*, 107.

57 **slave owners' treason:** McPherson, *Battle Cry*, 356, 500, 502.

57 **"forever free of the servitude":** Berlin et al., *Freedom*, 437.

57 **desert exile like the Mormons:** McPherson, *Battle Cry*, 145–46.

57 **"soft war" against slavery:** McPherson, *Antietam*, 67; Berlin et al., *Freedom*, 22; and Catton, *Never Call Retreat*, 56.

57 **July of 1862:** McPherson, *Tried by War*, 107.

57 **"impossible to foresee":** McPherson, *Antietam*, 65–66.

58 **Emancipation Proclamation:** McPherson, *Battle Cry*, 82–83, 117–45; Parrish, *History of Missouri*, 44, 94; McPherson, *Antietam*, 65; Goodwin, *Team of Rivals*, 566; Catton, *Never Call Retreat*, 113, 277, 427; and Fellman, *Inside War*, 69.

58 **"this species of property":** Berlin et al., *Freedom*, 723.

58 **"Either they labor for us":** Berlin et al., *Freedom*, 60.

58 **"nigger work":** Berlin et al., *Freedom*, 32.

58 **to find Negroes who would sign up:** Berlin et al., *Freedom*, 9, 28, 32, 36–38, 46, 111–12, 196, 260, 409, 411, 487–88, 500, 510, 664, 723; and Catton, *Never Call Retreat*, 114–15, 117, 510–11.

58 **until November of 1863:** Burke, *On Slavery's Border*, 292; and Fellman, *Inside War*, 213.

58 **owners locked up the shoes:** Berlin et al., *Freedom*, 409.

59 **"better than expected":** Robert K. Krick, *The American Civil War: The War in the East 1863–1865* (Oxford: Osprey Publishing, 2001), 59; and Berlin et al., *Freedom*, 13, 411.

59 **"cowardly rascals":** Krick, *American Civil War*, 59.

59 **Thirty-six soldiers:** SED 24, at 4; "Mower County Boys in Prison"; and "From the Ninth Regiment."

59 **Private James Woodbury:** Union Army, "Military Service Records—James Woodbury," NARA, College Park, Maryland; Basile, "Letters of a Minnesota Volunteer," 387–92; Minnesota GenWeb Project, "James M. Woodbury," at *Biographies: Mower County, Minnesota*, group file 22, RootsWeb.com, accessed August 2, 2009, http://rootsweb.ancestry

.com/~mnmower/bios/auxbio22.htm; and Adjutant General's Office, *Report of the Adjutant General*, 420–23.

60 **cartridge box as a desk**: Basile, "Letters of a Minnesota Volunteer," 441–42.

60 **Amanda Setzer**: Basile, "Letters of a Minnesota Volunteer," 387; and Inter-State Historical Company, *History of Mower County*, 214.

61 **What was the point now**: Basile, "Letters of a Minnesota Volunteer," 392, 438; Lord, *They Fought for the Union*, 200, 205; and Coggins, *Arms and Equipment*, 10.

61 **"kicked out of the Capitol"**: Basile, "Letters of a Minnesota Volunteer," 438.

61 **marching and drilling**: Basile, "Letters of a Minnesota Volunteer," 441.

61 **colder than Mower County**: Basile, "Letters of a Minnesota Volunteer," 442.

## 7. Captain Oscar B. Queen

63 **headed for the Otterville station**: SED 24, at 4; "Mower County Boys in Prison"; "From the Ninth Regiment"; Lord, *They Fought for the Union*, 47; and Johnson, *History of Cooper County*, 58, 61.

64 **war within the Civil War**: Burke, *On Slavery's Border*, 11, 272–73.

64 **"men seemed to have lost their reason"**: Johnson, *History of Cooper County*, 61.

64 **Sergeant Merchant split his detail**: SED 24, at 1; and Board of Commissioners, *Minnesota in the Civil and Indian Wars*, 419.

64 **half a dozen soldiers**: SED 24, at 4; and "From the Ninth Regiment."

65 **"You are at liberty to go your own way"**: Berlin et al., *Freedom*, 468.

66 **full cocked their rifles**: SED 24, at 1; and "The Rescue of Negroes in Missouri by Minnesota Soldiers," *Winona Daily Republican*, November 23, 1863.

66 **"By what authority"**: SED 24, at 1; "Rescue of Negroes in Missouri"; and NARA, *Letters Received*, JPG 2010–12.

67 **"Who is the officer in charge here?"**: SED 24, at 1–2.

67 **Queen wore an imposing officer's great coat**: NARA, *Letters Received*, JPG 2010–12.

68 **"We don't give a damn who you are!"**: NARA, *Letters Received*, JPG 2010–12.

68 **joined by another officer**: SED 24, at 2–3.

68 **direct orders from their commander**: NARA, *Letters Received*, JPG 1018, 2010–12.

68 **"until we get to the Lamine Bridge"**: "Rescue of Negroes in Missouri."

69 **it all sounded fine to him**: NARA, *"Letters Received*, JPG 2010–12.

69 **Oscar B. Queen was a native**: Oscar Eugene Queen to James Queen, August 20, 2004, courtesy of James Queen; "Queen-L Archives," Roots Web.com, accessed June 16, 2009, http://listsearches.rootsweb.com/th/read/QUEEN/2004-08/1094002439; James Queen to author, June 22, 2009, in the author's possession; Joseph Goldsborough Bruff, *Gold Rush: The Journals, Drawings, and Other Papers of J. Goldsborough Bruff, Captain, Washington City and California Mining Association, April 2, 1849–July 20, 1851* (Columbia NY: Columbia University Press, 1949), xxxix–liii, 1, 205, retrieved from the California Historical Society, San Francisco.

## 8. General Egbert Brown

71 **"Break for the woods"**: Berlin et al., *Freedom*, 468.

71 **hugged his wife and children**: "From the Ninth Regiment"; and SED 24, at 4.

71 **in a tight group around Merchant**: SED 24, at 4.

71 **"nigger catchers"**: Cornell, ser. 1, vol. 22, 548; and "Rescue of Negroes in Missouri."

72 **captured Union soldiers**: "Letter from Missouri," *Winona Daily Republican*, November 6–7, 1863.

72 **"We can take care of ourselves"**: SED 24, at 2.

72 **ran for the woods**: SED 24, at 4.

72 **they had a schedule to meet**: SED 24, at 2.

73 **Queen and Pritchard ordered the engineer**: NARA, *Letters Received*, JPG 1009; and Koenig, *Mars Gets New Chariots*, 75.

73 **The three men found their way to Captain Wellman's tent**: "Rescue of Negroes in Missouri."

73 **"I know nothing of this affair"**: SED 24, at 2.

74 **"The men are awol"**: SED 24, at 2.

74 **Wellman agreed to return**: SED 24, at 2.

74 **Bushwhackers often blocked**: Koenig, *Mars Gets New Chariots*, 73, 75.

75 **halfway back to Otterville**: NARA, *Letters Received*, JPG 1010, 1016–18; and SED 24, at 2.

75 **"Where are the Negroes?"**: SED 24, at 2.

76 **Early that night**: SED 24, at 2; NARA, *Letters Received*, JPG 2010–12; and Lord, *They Fought for the Union*, 90–91, 243.

76 **two slaves had sought safe harbor**: Berlin et al., *Freedom*, 430.

76 **a mellow violin sounded**: journal entry, January 10, 1863, John Aiton and Family Papers, MSHS.

76 **draft of a telegraph**: SED 24, at 2; and NARA, *Letters Received*, JPG 1014, 2010–12.

76 **General Brown was strongly pro-Union:** "Brigadier General Egbert Benson Brown," accessed January 3, 2010, http://www.history.missouristate .edu/battle_of_springfield/brigader_general_egbert_brown.htm (site now discontinued); *Wikipedia*, s.v. "Egbert B. Brown," accessed January 3, 2010, http://en.wikipedia.org/wiki/Egbert_B._Brown; "General Egbert Benson Brown, USA," Historycentral.com, accessed January 3, 2010, http://www.historycentral.com/Bio/UGENS/USABrown.html; SED 24, at 6; William S. Rosecrans to Abraham Lincoln, August 5, 1864, online at *The Abraham Lincoln Papers at the Library of Congress*, Manuscript Division (Washington DC: American Memory Project, 2000–2002), accessed January 3, 2010, http://memory.loc.gov/cgi-bin/query/P?mal:57:./ temp/~ammem_H3XU::@@@mdb= (site now discontinued).

77 **"a pinch of owl dung":** Michael Robert Patterson, "Samuel Davis Sturgis," Arlington National Cemetery Website, accessed March 9, 2010, www.arlingtoncemetery.net/ssturgis.htm.

77 **He began writing carefully:** SED 24, at 2; and Lord, *They Fought for the Union*, 237, 242.

77 **"give expression to individual feelings":** SED 24, at 2.

78 **"high-handed outrage":** SED 24, at 2, 4; and NARA, *Letters Received*, JPG 2010–12.

78 **ordering Captain Wellman to arrest the Minnesota soldiers:** NARA, *Letters Received*, JPG 1014.

78 **"desecrated vegetables":** Lord, *They Fought for the Union*, 120.

79 **"All parties who were engaged in the release":** SED 24, at 6; and NARA, *Letters Received*, JPG 1014.

79 **Thirty-six men:** "Mower County Boys in Prison"; SED 24, at 4. The exact number of men who were imprisoned is confusing. Newspaper accounts refer to "forty-one men." However, in a letter dated November 22, 1863, from C. S. Moore, assistant provost marshal at Jefferson City, he lists the names of seventeen men from Company C and eighteen men from Company K as the soldiers in prison awaiting trial. This totals thirty-five men, not counting Sergeant Merchant, who is not on the list but whose military service record indicates he was one of the imprisoned men. Thirty-six men, then, seems the most accurate number.

One explanation for the discrepancy could be that forty-one men did indeed participate in the rescue, but five men refused to step forward when Captain Wellman ordered the guilty parties to do so.

79 **"You are all under arrest":** SED 24, at 4; and Berlin et al., *Freedom*, 470.

79 **charged with mutiny:** SED 24, at 4.

## 9. Colonel Alexander Wilkin

80 **They boarded the same Pacific Railroad train:** NARA, *Letters Received*, JPG 1014; and "Mower County Boys in Prison."

80 **also sent a telegraph:** SED 24, at 2; and NARA, *Letters Received*, JPG 1006–1008.

80 **cocked their guns:** SED 24, at 2.

81 **basement of an abandoned:** "Mower County Boys in Prison"; "From the Ninth Regiment"; and Thomas and Hyman, *Stanton*, 244–45.

81 **"nominal, not real":** SED 24, at 4, 6.

81 **What would happen to them?:** Lord, *They Fought for the Union*, 208–11.

81 **Dry Tortugas:** Lord, *They Fought for the Union*, 208–11.

82 **tried by a general court-martial:** SED 24, at 4; Lord, *They Fought for the Union*, 111–13; and NARA, *Letters Received*, JPG 1013.

82 **What little food:** "Mower County Boys in Prison."

82 **The two warring factions:** "Armies in Motion," *New York Times*, November 9, 1863; "General Grant's Army," *New York Times*, November 8, 1863; and "Peace in Missouri," *New York Times*, November 29, 1863.

83 **"Another Nigger-Driver":** "Rescue of Negroes in Missouri"; and Astor, *Rebels on the Border*, 19, 77, 80, 87, 144, 210, 272.

83 **the little Pennsylvania town of Gettysburg:** Goodwin, *Team of Rivals*, 583–86; Steven Olson, *Lincoln's Gettysburg Address: A Primary Source Investigation* (New York: Rosen Publishing Group, 2009), 32; "The Heroic Dead at Gettysburg," *New York Times*, November 18, 1863; "National Cemetery Dedication," *New York Times*, November 19, 1863; "The Heroes of July," *New York Times*, November 20, 1863; and "The Gettysburg Celebration," *New York Times*, November 21, 1863.

84 **close by the slope:** Board of Commissioners, *Minnesota in the Civil and Indian Wars*, 34–37; and James A. Gross and Andrew Collins, *Gettysburg: The Souvenir Guide to the National Military Park* (Gettysburg: Tem, 1991).

85 **The men were to be commended, not jailed:** "Rescue of Negroes in Missouri."

85 **several men began crafting letters:** "Mower County Boys in Prison"; Board of Commissioners, *Minnesota in the Civil and Indian Wars*, 419; SED 24, at 3; and "Rescue of Negroes in Missouri."

86 **considered "indispensable":** Union Army, "Military Service Records—D. W. Wellman."

86 **he had been promoted to corporal:** Union Army, "Military Service Records—Henry Ehmke."

87 **cited his bold leadership:** "Mower County Boys in Prison."

87 **"ringleader's" directions:** NARA, *Letters Received*, JPG 2010.

87 "complete swindle": Basile, "Letters of a Minnesota Volunteer," 391–92.

87 hunt deer and turkeys: journal entry, December 15, 1862, John Aiton and Family Papers, MSHS.

## 10. Assemblyman H. J. Fisher

88 "noblest impulses of nature": "Rescue of Negroes in Missouri."

88 "learn to read and write": Berlin et al., *Freedom*, 475.

89 the names of the guilty soldiers: NARA, *Letters Received*, JPG 1013.

89 "heartfelt sympathies": SED 24, at 4.

89 pulled back from Richmond: "American Civil War December 1863," Historylearningsite.com, accessed May 28, 2012, http://www.historylearningsite.co.uk/december-1863-civil-war.htm.

89 no winter clothing: "American Civil War December 1863."

89 rats and mice disappeared: "Christmas 1863," Armchairgeneral.com, accessed May 28, 2012, http://www.armchairgeneral.com/christmas-1863.htm.

89 dramatic presentations: "Local Paragraphs," *Winona Daily Republican,* November 12, 13, 1863.

89 "boots and shoes": "New Store," *Mower County Register,* December 10, 1863.

89 turning in deserters: "Notice," *Mower County Register,* December 10, 1863.

89 "When will this war end?": "Christmas during the Civil War," Voices from the Past, accessed May 25, 2012, http://dburgin.tripod.com/cw_xmas/cwarxmas2.html.

89 "hirelings": "Letter from Missouri," *St. Paul Weekly Pioneer,* December 1863.

90 sketches that appeared: "Christmas," Awesomestories.com, accessed May 28, 2012, awesomestories.com/images/user/86ffed5eed.jpg; and "Life and the Civil War: 19th Century Christmas," Brotherswar.com, accessed May 28, 2012, http://brotherswar.com/Perspective-14.htm.

90 "chatting up treason": Bartels, *Civil War in Missouri,* 184–85.

90 Proclamation of Amnesty: "American Civil War December 1863."

90 immediately drafted a petition: SED 24, at 5; Berlin et al., *Freedom,* 468; and NARA, *Letters Received,* JPG 1018.

91 legislators reminded General Brown: NARA, *Letters Received,* JPG 1018.

91 fired back a letter: SED 24, at 5; Berlin et al., *Freedom,* 470; and NARA, *Letters Received,* JPG 998–1001.

92 Fisher dashed off another letter: SED 24, at 5–6.

92 Brown's constituency: *Wikipedia,* s.v. "Benjamin Gratz Brown," accessed January 3, 2010, http://en.wikipedia.org/wiki/B._Gratz_Brown.

92 letter on behalf of the soldiers: SED 24, at 6.

92 **General Brown gave ground grudgingly:** SED 24, at 6.

93 **his own investigation:** SED 24, at 6.

93 **they were sorry:** Berlin et al., *Freedom*, 470; SED 24, at 7; and NARA, *Letters Received*, JPG 998–1001.

## 11. Senator Morton Wilkinson

95 **the Potomac River froze:** "News from Washington," *New York Times*, January 11, 1864.

95 **a week of "elegant parties":** "From Washington," *New York Times*, January 13, 1864.

95 **Vice President Hannibal Hamlin:** Wikipedia, s.v. "Hannibal Hamlin," accessed January 5, 2010, http://en.wikipedia.org/wiki/Hannibal _Hamlin; *Cong. Globe*, 38th Cong., 1st Sess., January 13, 1864, 145–46 (hereafter *Globe*); and *Globe*, March 29, 1864, 1317, 1319.

96 **portion of Texas:** *Globe*, January 13, 1864, 145–46.

96 **Constitutional amendment to abolish slavery:** *Globe*, January 13, 1864, 145.

97 **Senator Morton Wilkinson:** *Globe*, January 13, 1864, 145–46; SED 24, at 1; *Globe*, March 29, 1864, 1317, 1319; Board of Commissioners, *Minnesota in the Civil and Indian Wars*, 420; and "Wilkinson, Morton Smith," Minnesota State Legislature, accessed January 3, 2010, http://www.leg .state.mn.us/legdb/fulldetail.aspx?ID=11956.

97 **"is hereby instructed":** *Globe*, January 13, 1864, 145; Board of Commissioners, *Minnesota in the Civil and Indian Wars*, 420; and Wikipedia, s.v. "38th United States Congress," accessed March 8, 2010, http:// en.wikipedia.org/wiki/38th_United_States_Congress.

97 **All eyes turned to Wilkinson for the details:** *Globe*, January 13, 1864, 145.

98 **"These things in the state of Missouri must stop!":** *Globe*, January 13, 1864, 145.

99 **"as good a regiment as could be found":** *Globe*, January 13, 1864, 145.

99 **"some little act of insubordination":** *Globe*, January 13, 1864, 145.

99 **"the tools of slavery-loving tyrants":** *Globe*, January 13, 1864, 145.

99 **James Henry Lane:** "James Henry Lane, 1814–1866," *Territorial Kansas Online*, accessed June 9, 2009, http://www.territorialkansasonline .org/~imlskto/cgi-bin/index.php?SCREEN=bio_sketches/lane_james; and SED 24, at 7.

100 **"scores if not hundreds of soldiers":** *Globe*, January 13, 1864, 145.

100 **Charles Sumner:** Wikipedia, s.v. "28th United States Congress," accessed January 3, 2010, http://en.wikipedia.org/wiki/28th _United_States_Congress.

100 **"By whose order?"**: *Globe*, January 13, 1864, 145.

101 **"I desire the resolution be passed"**: *Globe*, January 13, 1864, 146.

## 12. General John McAlister Schofield

102 **the president had anguished**: Goodwin, *Team of Rivals*, 349, 365, 388–89, 511, 566–67; McPherson, *Battle Cry*, 290–93; Catton, *Never Call Retreat*, 109; Fellman, *Inside War*, 84–89, 95, 110; Bartels, *Civil War in Missouri*, 48; Parrish, *History of Missouri*, 4, 31, 35, 43, 56–57, 62–63, 69–70, 94, 103, 109; Carley, *Sioux Uprising*, 63–67; and Gallagher, *American Civil War*, 81.

102 **unhandy "devils"**: Goodwin, *Team of Rivals*, 567.

102 **"I have been tormented"**: Parrish, *History of Missouri*, 57.

102 **"I am compelled"**: Goodwin, *Team of Rivals*, 511.

103 **one general after another**: McPherson, *Battle Cry*, 351–52; Goodwin, *Team of Rivals*, 390–91, 406; Fellman, *Inside War*, 65; Bartels, *Civil War in Missouri*, 20; Parrish, *History of Missouri*, 28–29, 33, 36, 38, 45, 57, 59, 98; and McPherson, *Tried by War*, 60.

103 **"too difficult a task"**: "Gen. Rosecrans Again in Command," *New York Times*, February 4, 1864.

103 **"It is not for me"**: "Gen. Rosecrans Again in Command."

103 **Major General John McAlister Schofield**: Wikipedia, s.v. "John Schofield," accessed January 8, 2010, http://en.wikipedia.org/wiki/John _Schofield; and "News from Washington," *New York Times*, December 15, 1863.

104 **"Does not General Schofield understand?"**: "The Arrested Minnesota Soldiers," *St. Paul Pioneer Weekly*, December 24, 1863; and "Mower County Boys in Prison."

104 **"slavery's fools"**: "The Right Move at Last," *Mower County Register*, January 21, 1864.

104 **"Sleighing is splendid"**: "Affairs in Missouri," *New York Times*, January 7, 1864.

## 13. Secretary of War Edwin M. Stanton

106 **"that damned long-armed ape"**: Goodwin, *Team of Rivals*, 175, 560.

106 **"the rock on the beach"**: Thomas and Hyman, *Stanton*, 384, 386, 394; and Goodwin, *Team of Rivals*, 115–17, 559–62, 668–72

106 **left their camp in the bitter cold at the Lamine Bridge**: Basile, "Letters of a Minnesota Volunteer," 443; Board of Commissioners, *Minnesota in the Civil and Indian Wars*, 418; "Letter from General E. B. Brown to Dr. S. H. Saunders," January 4, 1864, Cornell, ser. 1, vol. 22.

106 **Jesse James burned the bridge:** Denny, "Civil War Entrenchment," 7.

106 **headed west for Warrensburg:** Basile, "Letters of a Minnesota Volunteer," 443; and Board of Commissioners, *Minnesota in the Civil and Indian Wars*, 418.

107 **rebuilding and guarding another bridge:** Basile, "Letters of a Minnesota Volunteer," 443.

107 **"to the great annoyance of citizens":** E. H. Couse to Lieutenant Waschman, February 12, 1864, in *Regimental Letters*.

107 **Irishman was shot in the head:** Basile, "Letters of a Minnesota Volunteer," 443-44.

107 **"like spring again":** Basile, "Letters of a Minnesota Volunteer," 443.

107 **relieve his aging father:** Freeborn County Minnesota AHGP, "'History of Freeborn County,' 1882"; and Inter-State Historical Company, *History of Mower County*, 150–51, 163, 213–14.

108 **permanent place in Winona's commerce:** Basile, "Letters of a Minnesota Volunteer," 443; and Winona County Historical Society, *River Town Winona*, v, 7, 9.

109 **had been a short rendezvous:** Basile, "Letters of a Minnesota Volunteer," 387; Inter-State Historical Company, *History of Mower County*, 208, 218; Torgrimson, "Of Days that Used to Be," 4; and Basile, "Letters of a Minnesota Volunteer," 443-44.

109 **"he better send us home":** Basile, "Letters of a Minnesota Volunteer," 443-44.

109 **a bridge building expert:** Union Army, "Military Service Records—D. W. Wellman."

109 **hector his superiors:** Union Army, "Military Service Records—D. W. Wellman."

109 **an audience with General Ulysses S. Grant:** Hubbs, "Civil War and Alexander Wilkin," 185; "Letter from Missouri," *St. Paul Pioneer Weekly*, February 4, 1864.

109 **He had earned a reputation as an aggressive commander:** *Wikipedia*, s.v. "Ulysses S. Grant," accessed May 1, 2012, http://en.wikipedia.org/wiki/Ulysses_S._Grant.

110 **if he knew Grant's brand of whiskey:** McPherson, *Battle Cry*, 588.

110 **"feted and petted":** "Letter from Missouri," *St. Paul Pioneer Weekly*, February 4, 1864.

110 **"looked upon as something wonderful":** Hubbs, "Civil War and Alexander Wilkin," 184-85.

110 **"I would very much like to have you with me":** Hubbs, "Civil War and Alexander Wilkin," 185.

110 "the first man shot": Basile, "Letters of a Minnesota Volunteer," 443.

110 Secretary Stanton continued to put together the report: SED 24, at 108; and NARA, *Letters Received*, JPG 997–1001, JPG 1004–9, JPG 1013–18, JPG 2010–12.

111 fighting for his life: Cornell, ser. 1, vol. 41, 356–57, 364–65; Federal Publishing, ed., *The Union Army: A History of Military Affairs in the Loyal States, 1861–65* (Madison WI: Federal Publishing, 1908), 6:781; and Demuth, *History of Pettis County*, 386–90.

111 "not again take up arms": Thomas and Hyman, *Stanton*, 372–73.

112 fresh war news: "Reports from Washington," *New York Times*, March 4, 1864; "Army of the Potomac," *New York Times*, March 4, 1864; "From Washington," *New York Times*, March 5, 1864; and "From the Southwest," *New York Times*, March 4, 1864.

112 "cattle in a slaughter pen": "From Washington," *New York Times*, March 5, 1864.

112 an eight-page letter: Thomas and Hyman, *Stanton*, 384, 386, 394; Goodwin, *Team of Rivals*, 114, 175, 177, 669; and McPherson, *Tried by War*, 102.

113 what was in this report: *Globe*, March 4, 1864, 936; and SED 24, at 1.

113 "The man must die": Goodwin, *Team of Rivals*, 671.

113 "lie on the table": SED 24, at 1.

113 "the man in a hurry": Thomas and Hyman, *Stanton*, 381.

114 formal military charges had been drawn up: "Arrested Minnesota Soldiers"; NARA, *Letters Received*, JPG 997, JPG 1003, JPG 1015; Berlin et al., 469–70; and SED 24, at 1–8.

114 contained a letter from a private: SED 24, at 1–8.

115 The report included other letters: SED 24, at 108; and NARA, *Letters Received*, JPG 997–1001, JPG 1004–9, JPG 1013–18, JPG 2010–12.

115 Those who volunteered: SED 24, at 5.

116 Brown was adamant in his disagreement: SED 24, at 4–7.

116 "trumped up charge": SED 24, at 6.

116 "The application by General Brown": SED 24, at 7.

116 "The interests of the service": SED 24, at 1.

## 14. Taps

117 scattered elements of the Ninth: Board of Commissioners, *Minnesota in the Civil and Indian Wars*, 420.

117 eight thousand–man force: Board of Commissioners, *Minnesota in the Civil and Indian Wars*, 420.

117 "Ladies' Great Sanitary Fair": Board of Commissioners, *Minnesota in the Civil and Indian Wars*, 420; Maine Memory Network, "Ladies Sani-

tary Fair Fundraiser, Bangor, 1864," www.mainememory.net (accessed
January 20, 2010).

118 **marched south through rain:** Board of Commissioners, *Minnesota in
the Civil and Indian Wars*, 420–21; and Hubbs, "Civil War and Alexander
Wilkin," 186.

118 **topographic engineer in Missouri:** Board of Commissioners, *118 in the
Civil and Indian Wars*, 192; Union Army, "Military Service Records—D.
W. Wellman"; and Cornell, ser. 2, vol. 1, 230.

118 **Wellman was a "good officer":** Union Army, "Military Service Records—D. W. Wellman."

118 **relieved of his command of the Central District of Missouri:** *Wikipedia*, s.v. "Egbert B. Brown," accessed January 3, 2010, http://en.wikipedia
.org/wiki/Egbert_B._Brown.

118–119 **Brice's Crossroads in northern Mississippi:** Board of Commissioners, *Minnesota in the Civil and Indian Wars*, 421–26; Basile, "Letters
of a Minnesota Volunteer," 338; and Hubbs, "Civil War and Alexander
Wilkin," 187–88.

120 **passed around a bottle of whiskey:** Board of Commissioners, *Minnesota in the Civil and Indian Wars*, 422.

120 **a train for Memphis:** Board of Commissioners, *Minnesota in the Civil
and Indian Wars*, 424.

120–121 **just north of Tupelo:** Board of Commissioners, *Minnesota in the
Civil and Indian Wars*, 410, 427.

121 **He fell to the ground:** Board of Commissioners, *Minnesota in the Civil and Indian Wars*, 426–27, 439; and Hubbs, "Civil War and Alexander
Wilkin," 174, 190.

122 **his last letters:** Board of Commissioners, *Minnesota in the Civil and Indian Wars*, 427; and Hubbs, "Civil War and Alexander Wilkin," 189.

122 **"slowly and in fine order":** Board of Commissioners, *Minnesota in the
Civil and Indian Wars*, 421.

122 **Woodbury was captured:** Board of Commissioners, *Minnesota in the Civil and Indian Wars*, 424; Union Army, "Military Service Records—James
Woodbury"; and Basile, "Letters of a Minnesota Volunteer," 446.

122–123 **Andersonville, Georgia:** Raymond Baker, *Andersonville: The Story
of a Civil War Prison Camp* (Washington DC: National Park Service, 1972),
2–4, 7, 9–10, 12–13, 18–20.

123 **he was admitted:** Union Army, "Military Service Records—James Woodbury"; Captain H. R. Hubbard, "Andersonville Hospital Conditions,"
JanneyFamily.com, accessed January 22, 2010, http://www.janney
family.com/harmon_hubbard/hr_civil_war_02_04; and Basile, "Letters
of a Minnesota Volunteer," 388.

123 his heart stopped: Basile, "Letters of a Minnesota Volunteer," 446.

123 delivered their first child: Basile, "Letters of a Minnesota Volunteer," 388.

123 "If I had known as much": Basile, "Letters of a Minnesota Volunteer," 392.

124 "alone and uncared for": Basile, "Letters of a Minnesota Volunteer," 445–46.

124 a paper ticket identifying: *St. Paul Pioneer Press*, January 7, 1865.

124 "bivouac for the dead": Inter-State Historical Company, *History of Mower County*, 198; Hubbard, "Anderson Hospital Conditions"; and "Return of the Andersonville Burial Party," *New York Times*, August 25, 1865.

124 without coffins: "Return of the Andersonville Burial Party," *New York Times*, August 25, 1865.

124 all of the Union dead: "From Washington," *New York Times*, August 12, 1865; and "From Washington," *New York Times*, August 13, 1865.

124 "galaxy of beauty and fashion": "The Grand Two-Mile Race for Three-Year-Olds," *New York Times*, August 12, 1865.

125 There were banquets and celebrations: Trenerry, "Minnesota Rebellion Act," 191–92.

125 Citizens lined the river banks: Board of Commissioners, *Minnesota in the Civil and Indian Wars*, 436–37.

125 infected wounds, hearing loss: Winona County Historical Society, "Green Book: Civil War Pension Documents," (finding aid, Winona MN: Winona County Historical Society).

125 fought bravely at Tupelo: Union Army, "Military Service Records—Henry Ehmke"; "Henry Ehmke, Civil War Veteran," *Winona Republican-Herald*, March 11, 1929; and Board of Commissioners, *Minnesota in the Civil and Indian Wars*, 429.

126 "indolent" soldiering: Trenerry, "When the Boys Came Home," *Minnesota History Magazine* 38, no. 6 (June 1963): 291–92.

126 his new bride: "Henry Ehmke, Civil War Veteran."

126 opened a butcher shop: "Henry Ehmke, Civil War Veteran."

126 had his foot torn off: "Henry Ehmke, Civil War Veteran."

127 He died in 1929: "Henry Ehmke, Civil War Veteran."

127 spent two months in the hospital: Union Army, "Military Service Records—James Merchant."

127 sent to defend Nashville: Union Army, "Military Service Records—James Merchant"; and Board of Commissioners, *Minnesota in the Civil and Indian Wars*, 430.

127 "Minnesota! Minnesota!": Board of Commissioners, *Minnesota in the Civil and Indian Wars*, 431–432.

127 **promoted once more:** Union Army, "Military Service Records—James Merchant"; Freeborn County Minnesota AHGP, "'History of Freeborn County,' 1882"; and Board of Commissioners, *Minnesota in the Civil and Indian Wars*, 436.

128 **Decoration Day:** "Sermon of Rev. C. E. Wright," *Mower County Transcript*, June 17, 1880.

128 **"The world had never seen such an army":** "Sermon of Rev. C. E. Wright."

128 **"honest men, good citizens":** "Died: Frank Koelmel," *Wabasha Herald*, May 3, 1884; and "Thomas Morton Dead," *Wabasha Herald*, September 12, 1912.

128 **"made of sound sense":** "The Few Who Have Doubted," *Freeborn County Standard*, May 26, 1886; "Frank Merchant of Oakland," *Freeborn County Standard*, November 14, 1883; "Frank Merchant," *Freeborn County Standard*," May 5, 1886; and "Mrs. Francis Merchant."

128 **"inefficient, incompetent, evil":** "C. D. Fuller Claims Ten Thousand Dollars Damages," *Freeborn County Standard*, December 19, 1888; "The Friends of Frank Merchant," *Freeborn County Standard*, January 24, 1889; and "Friends of Frank Merchant," *Freeborn County Standard*, May 30, 1889.

128 **moved to Minneapolis:** "Ex Chief-of-Police Frank Merchant," *Freeborn County Standard*, April 4, 1889.

129 **served as president:** "The Old Ninth," *Minneapolis Journal*, February 23, 1899.

129 **his wife of forty six years:** "Mrs. Francis Merchant."

129 **Sunday, October 1, 1927:** "Merchant, Francis," *Austin Daily Herald*, October 24, 1927.

129 **slugger Babe Ruth:** "Sixtieth of 1927 Season," *Oakland Tribune*, October 1, 1927.

129 **body was returned to Austin:** "Merchant, Francis."

129 **there was no marker:** visit to Oakwood Cemetery by the author, July 19, 2009.

129 **"There's a lot of 'em":** Oakwood Cemetery manager, in conversation with the author, July 19, 2009.

130 **respectable and promising family:** U.S. Bureau of the Census, *1870 Census, Pettis County, Missouri* (Washington DC: Bureau of the Census, 1870), 797.

130 **laborers:** U.S. Bureau of the Census, *1870 Census, Pettis County, Missouri*, 797.

130 **Freedman's Relief Bureau:** Berlin et al., *Freedom*, 47–48, 270–76, 411, 471; and "Freedman's Relief Meeting," *New York Times*, February 27, 1864.

130 **"fierce on the track":** "Rescue of Negroes in Missouri."

130 **"crafty and cunning":** Harriet Frazier, *Runaway and Freed Missouri Slaves*,

and Those Who Helped Them, *1763–1865* (Jefferson NC: McFarland, 2004), 88, 93.

130 **"how long are we going to be cursed"**: Berlin et al., *Freedom*, 477; and Stowe, *Uncle Tom's Cabin*, 88–89, 333, 341.

130 **"bid him strike for the human race"**: Thomas and Hyman, *Stanton*, 133.

130 **200,000 freed slaves**: Lord, *They Fought for the Union*, 17; Berlin et al., *Freedom*, 46; Burke, *On Slavery's Border*, 292; and Astor, *Rebels on the Border*, 104, 124–25.

130 **nearly 4,000**: Astor, *Rebels on the Border*, 174.

131 **"damn abolitionist scheme"**: Berlin et al., *Freedom*, 410, 477; and "Gen. Butler and the Blacks," *New York Times*, December 12, 1863.

131 **"We have a right to do what we please"**: "Employment of Free Negroes and Slaves," *New York Times*, January 31, 1864.

131 **slept in barns by day**: *Wikipedia*, s.v. "Underground Railroad," accessed January 20, 2010, http://en.wikipedia.org/wiki/Underground_Railroad; Frazier, *Runaway and Freed Missouri Slaves*, 113, 174–75; and Astor, *Rebels on the Border*, 126.

CPSIA information can be obtained at www.ICGtesting.com
Printed in the USA
BVOW02s1556061013

332855BV00007B/1/P